On the edge

a study of poverty and long-term
unemployment in Northern Ireland

Eileen Evason

Published by Child Poverty Action Group
1 Macklin Street, London WC2B 5NH

Eileen Evason is Lecturer in Social Administration at the
New University of Ulster and a member of CPAG (NI)

© Child Poverty Action Group 1985
ISBN 0 903963 91 4

*The views expressed in this publication are not necessarily
those of Child Poverty Action Group*

Cover design by Susan Hobbs
Typeset by Nancy White
Printed by Calvert's North Star Press (TU), London

Contents

1 Introduction   1
2 Northern Ireland's social security system   4
3 Dependence and key benefits   13
4 Groups at risk   19
5 The Derry survey: background   34
6 General characteristics   37
7 Unemployment: past, present and future   39
8 Living standards: past and present   42
9 Some other consequences of unemployment   50
10 Perceptions, attitudes and life styles   53
11 Aspects of the benefits system   61
12 Conclusion   64

Acknowledgements

This report is the result of the efforts of many members of CPAG (NI). Pat Armstrong must take much of the credit for seeing the project through. He was responsible for doing most of the interviewing and demonstrated extraordinary perseverance, humour and common sense throughout. Rose Logue assisted with the interviews and preparation of some of the statistical material for this report. Danny Breslin provided constant support and back up for the fieldwork, as did Kathleen McPartland, Sally Quinn and Eamonn McTernan. CPAG (NI) is grateful to the Northern Ireland Voluntary Trust and Derry City Council for the financial assistance which enabled us to undertake the work. Above all, we are grateful to the people of Derry who supported and participated in the project.

We would also like to thank Hilary Arnott, of CPAG, and Nancy White for their help in producing this pamphlet, as well as Fran Bennett, Ruth Lister, Peter Townsend and Paul Wilding for their constructive comments.

Eileen Evason
November 1985

1 Introduction

Northern Ireland has a population of one and a half million. The two main cities are Belfast, with a population of approximately 300,000, and Derry, at the other end of the province, with a population of roughly 83,000. It is indicative of the difficulties of the region that even this most basic information cannot be entirely relied upon. Considerable controversy, and some violence, surrounded the 1981 census, and under-reporting was a significant problem — particularly in Catholic areas.

For the past 16 years, the province has experienced what we still euphemistically describe as 'the troubles'. Atrocities have been perpetrated by all the participants to the conflict, which has gone through many stages. There are, however, many sides to Northern Ireland. Some areas are perpetually embattled, whilst in many others life appears to be, and indeed is, quite normal.

For the past 13 years, the province has been under direct rule from Westminster. The job of Secretary of State for Northern Ireland is considered one of the least desirable in British politics. However, the junior posts have given some ministers a chance to shine and, with varying degrees of energy, our visiting politicians have bent their minds to the formidable social and economic problems of the province.

The problems are not new, and precede the present conflict. The position prior to the onset of 'the troubles' has been most ably summarised by Peter Townsend:

> In my first visit to Belfast in 1968 (incidentally, just before the disorder and bloodshed that has persisted right through the 1970s), I was struck not only by the evident poverty in Catholic and Protestant areas alike, but by scenes which seemed to belong more to the 1930s — of red-haired boys using scales on a cart drawn by an emaciated pony to sell coal by the pound, teenage girls in a second-hand clothing shop buying underslips and skirts, and some of the smallest 'joints' of meat in butchers' windows that I have ever seen. Here, as in the other areas, working conditions, housing and the immediate environment of the home were often raw and harsh. This is not to say, of course, that there were not also some superbly laid-out and kept homes, shops and workshops. But, by various of our measures, the deprivation in

these areas was undeniable. Over two-thirds of families with children in the four areas had insufficient bedroom space, and over two-thirds declared that there was no safe place for their young children to play in near the home. Nearly two-thirds of all homes were said to suffer from structural defects, and as many as 86 per cent of the working men interviewed in the second stage of our surveys were found to have poor or bad working conditions (compared with 21 per cent in the United Kingdom as a whole).[1]

In Townsend's survey, 44.3% of Northern Ireland's households were classified as in poverty and the region was clearly the most deprived in the UK. Whilst in crude terms living standards have improved significantly in Northern Ireland since 1968/9, in relative terms the province retains its unenviable position as the most disadvantaged region in the UK, and the percentage of households in poverty is unlikely to have altered much. The province remains trapped, as later sections of this pamphlet demonstrate, by its own special combination of handicaps: lower wages, higher prices and the worst unemployment rate of any UK region. The result is lower household incomes which must be stretched even further as households are slightly larger in Northern Ireland than elsewhere.

Ten years ago, CPAG published *Poverty: the facts in Northern Ireland*.[2] In recognition of the continuing situation of acute deprivation, *On the edge* updates the data presented then and summarises the considerable developments in research that have occurred over the past decade. In addition, it presents the results of a recently completed survey of the unemployed in two communities in Derry, carried out by CPAG (Northern Ireland). This survey, the largest and most detailed examination of the circumstances of the unemployed to be carried out in this part of the UK, illuminates many of the issues highlighted in the first part of the pamphlet.

The purpose of this report is not, however, a merely descriptive one. It is hoped that, rather than being seen purely as a depressing litany of facts from a remote region — deserving of sympathy, but nevertheless peripheral to discussions of poverty and policy on the mainland — the data presented will be interpreted as of relevance to analysis and discussion of what is happening across the UK as a whole.

It is perhaps surprising that, despite the considerable knowledge and experience gained in Northern Ireland over the past decade, so little of it has been integrated into general theory and analysis. Northern Ireland is still treated as separate and different, yet in recent years many parts of Britain have been scarred by social disorder and experienced the effects of deindustrialisation. At the same time, the current upsurge of interest in Britain in the connection between racism and social policy echoes the experience of Northern Ireland, for housing allocation policy was at the heart of the events surrounding the onset of the conflict in Northern Ireland in the late 1960s which has continued to the present day.

The parallels cannot be pushed too far, but it can be argued that, at least to some extent, Northern Ireland is not a special case but a test case. No other region in the UK so clearly demonstrates that low wages, high unemployment and 'good' industrial relations are not the path to economic prosperity. No other region in the UK demonstrates so clearly the diversity of ends which the social security system can serve. No other region demonstrates so clearly the potential of social policies for integrating — or alienating — minorities. No other region demonstrates so clearly that the social security system can preside over, cope with and contain levels of need previously thought unimaginable — and then impose cuts in addition. No other region demonstrates so clearly the inadequacy and irrelevance of the Green Paper, *Reform of Social Security*[3] (published while this report was being written), to the problem of poverty in the UK. Above all, no other region so effectively refutes the view that, over time, individuals, families and communities can adjust to poverty line incomes and unemployment and find ways of coping with the financial, social and psychological costs of income deprivation and worklessness.

To demonstrate this, *On the edge* reviews the social security system in general in Northern Ireland, analyses statistical information relating to key benefits, assesses the data available relating to groups at risk of income deprivation, and outlines the results of the survey of the unemployed in Derry city conducted in 1983/4.

References

1 P Townsend, *Poverty in the United Kingdom*, Penguin 1979, p 558.
2 E Evason, *Poverty: the facts in Northern Ireland*, CPAG 1976.
3 *The Reform of Social Security*, Vol 1, Cmnd 9517, London HMSO 1985.

2 Northern Ireland's social security system

Despite its separate legal base, at first glance the benefits system in Northern Ireland appears to follow that of Britain fairly closely. National insurance benefits are in fact identical, with Northern Ireland claimants being entitled to the same benefits on the same conditions for the same contributions. There are, however, differences in connection with some of the other benefits provided and in the impact and effect of the system as a whole.

Responsibility for the majority of benefits is carried by the Northern Ireland Department of Health and Social Services and a network of local offices; there are no regional offices. Local offices in Northern Ireland administer unemployment benefit but not sickness and maternity benefit or retirement and widow's pensions. Thus, the administration of non-means-tested benefits is more centralised in Northern Ireland. The administration of many means-tested benefits also differs from arrangements in Britain. This is a consequence of the fact that local government in Northern Ireland bears little resemblance to the British structure — though again, some interesting parallels are emerging.

In the early 1970s, the eight major local authorities in Northern Ireland were abolished and replaced by 26 district councils with minimal powers. Responsibility for housing, health, personal social services and education was transferred to a series of bodies whose members are appointed by central government. Thus, responsibility for building, allocating and managing public housing was transferred to the Northern Ireland Housing Executive. The Department of the Environment directly administers services such as planning, roads, water and sewerage through a network of local offices. Four Area Boards are responsible, as agents of the DHSS, for health and personal social services and, similarly, under the Department of Education (NI), there are five Education and Library Boards.

The main result of these arrangements is that benefits which are administered by local authorities in the rest of the UK are more directly under the control of non-elected bodies in Northern Ireland. Thus, benefits for school children are administered by the Education and Library Boards, and housing benefit is, in fact, administered by three central bodies: the Northern Ireland Housing Executive, the Department of the Environment and the DHSS.

Moreover, since the introduction of direct rule, the ministers

4

responsible have been appointed by Westminster, and the only regional elected body — the Northern Ireland Assembly — has a purely advisory function. It can thus be argued that the system of welfare benefits as it has developed over the past 15 years in Northern Ireland is more centralised and subject to rather more remote control than the structure in Britain.

Despite these differences in administration, the stated principle underlying the Northern Ireland structure of benefits throughout the post-war period has been that of parity with Britain. The precise meaning of this concept is, however, elusive — indeed, on occasion it has almost appeared as though the concept is deployed when it suits government's purposes and disregarded when it does not. The principle of parity was, for example, a central plank in the argument for the introduction of the housing benefit scheme into Northern Ireland: the scheme was introduced a year later than in Britain and much of the general argument in its favour lacked credibility by that stage. The concept of parity has, however, proved elastic enough to encompass a number of departures from British provision — sometimes to Northern Ireland's advantage and sometimes not.

In effect, parity appears to mean providing more or less (though not quite) the same benefits — but disregarding differences in the actual impact of these benefits produced by broader policies and problems, and retaining the freedom to introduce ancillary measures. These measures do not overtly alter the system, but in practice produce significant departures in its functions and objectives — and perhaps in local perceptions of the benefits system.

The main differences in benefits relate to housing benefit and supplementary benefit (SB). On housing benefit, as a result of pressure from the Assembly, a number of minor improvements on the British scheme have been introduced. Thus, there is a statutory obligation to make the first payment of housing benefit 'where practicable' within 14 days of all relevant information being received in standard as well as certificated cases. In Britain, the obligation covers certificated cases only. In addition, the Executive has no power to recover overpayments due to official error in standard cases. At the same time, boarders on SB can claim housing benefit for up to four weeks for accommodation not yet occupied and the Executive has discretionary powers to make interim payments where full entitlement cannot be determined. On the credit side, also, water rates are eligible for rebate in Northern Ireland.

In practice, the value of many of these concessions is debatable. It should also be noted that the Assembly formally rejected the government's scheme and proposed instead a more radical no-loser scheme for Northern Ireland. In addition, at the time of the introduction of the scheme (1983), there was considerable pressure for

5

Northern Ireland to be declared a 'High Rent Area' in the light of the staggering rent increases in the public sector which had just been imposed by government. In Northern Ireland, rents rose by 26% in 1980, 38% in 1981 and 22% in 1982, causing particular hardship in a low wage economy. Nevertheless, Northern Ireland was not declared a High Rent Area. There is, in fact, no provision for declaring such areas within Northern Ireland, though provision does exist for classes of dwellings to have this label attached. Nor is there any provision corresponding to the power accorded to British authorities to enhance the basic scheme by 10%.

With regard to the SB scheme, there are two main differences between British and Northern Irish provision. First, under Article 8 of the Supplementary Benefit (Northern Ireland) Order 1977, there is an exclusion from benefit of persons not resident in the UK for the five years preceding the claim. The Article is modified by the Supplementary Benefit (Conditions of Entitlement) Regulations (Northern Ireland) 1981, so that the exclusion effectively applies only to non-UK citizens apart from refugees.* This provision is of interest for two reasons. First, it constitutes a possible precedent for the 'presence test' which the Green Paper suggests will be attached to the income support scheme when it replaces SB. Second, it can be argued that Northern Ireland's provision is patently discriminatory on grounds of nationality, and is therefore in direct conflict with EEC law (Article 7(2) 1612/68), which prohibits member states from treating workers from other member states differently with regard to social and tax advantages.

The other respect in which Northern Ireland's SB scheme differs from that of Britain relates to debt. The Northern Ireland regulations allow for direct payment of unrebated rent (Executive tenants only) and rates. In other words, if claimants fail to hand over the amounts grown-up children in the household are assumed to be giving them under the housing benefit scheme, these amounts can be deducted at source from the claimant's SB. Direct payment can also be used for amenity charges such as fuel. These provisions have a particular significance in Northern Ireland because families are larger and more likely to contain non-dependent children, and there is a greater dependence on high cost district heating.

It is of interest that, in its evidence to the Health and Social Services Committee of the Assembly on Parity, the DHSS(NI) justified this departure from British provision on the grounds that it was designed to prevent claimants from getting into arrears and becoming subject to 'benefit allocation'.[2] Benefit allocation itself, ~ever, is peculiar to Northern Ireland. Hence, one departure from ~y has been justified by reference to another — the notorious

*ing aside countries with which there are reciprocal agreements.

1971 Payments for Debt (Emergency Provisions) Act (Northern Ireland).

The Payments for Debt Act is still in force and has played a critical role in government's response to two quite distinct problems. The Act was introduced as an emergency measure to deal with a specific political problem — the withholding of rent and rates which followed internment. The Act not only allowed money to be deducted at source from the benefits of people in arrears to public bodies, but also provided for charges to be levied to cover the cost of collection. At the same time, those subject to benefit allocation were excluded from receipt of exceptional needs payments and had no right of appeal when such payments were refused under these provisions.[3]

In the latter part of the 1970s, changes were made in the operation of the Act, removing some of its worst aspects; but it was, nevertheless, not only retained but extended in scope, so that deductions could also be made from the wages of public employees and in respect of fuel debts. Internment and the rent and rates strike were over by this time, and the justification for the extension, rather than repeal, of the Act was that the level of debt in Northern Ireland was extraordinarily high and, to a significant extent, the consequence of wilful refusal to pay. Both points were strongly contested and there was little evidence for this position. As Table 1 indicates, Northern Ireland's rent arrears, in the period preceding the introduction of the housing benefit scheme, do not appear remarkable when comparisons are made with similarly deprived areas. Moreover, substantial research has demonstrated that debt is the inevitable consequence of Northern Ireland's higher prices and lower incomes (and this has been accepted publicly by the Executive).

Table 1: *Rent arrears for Northern Ireland and selected London boroughs (1982)*

Borough	Current tenants	% in arrears	Av arrears per tenant
Haringey	25,573	51.7	£231.64
Brent	21,901	54.3	£163.05
Southwark	62,551	30.4	£138.28
Lambeth	45,006	68.1	£132.22
Wandsworth	38,118	65.5	£102.38
Hackney	45,000	53.7	£102.38
Camden	35,060	50.1	£97.34
NI Housing Executive	186,055	58.6	£89.46

Source: D Graham, *The Cutting Edge*, North Belfast Community Resource Centre 1985

In essence, therefore, the Payments for Debt Act has been used since the latter part of the 1970s to ensure that the province's rising rents and fuel prices result in private hardship rather than public debt. Deductions can still be made at source from all major benefits and allowances, including, in some circumstances, child benefit. Low paid workers in public employment can still have their wages docked when in debt. In such cases, the maximum deduction is supposed to be £11.45 per week, but errors are not unknown — and even without error the results can be devastating. In one recent case, for example, £54.81 was deducted from an employee's gross wage of £69.19!

In 1983/4, the total cost of operating the Payments for Debt Act was nearly half a million pounds, and it constitutes a useful additional measure for dealing with claimants not on SB.[4] More broadly, it is also worth noting that a measure similar to the Payments for Debt Act may have to be introduced on the mainland from 1987 to recover loans made under the proposed social fund.

Thus, the social security system in Northern Ireland has become, to a greater extent than elsewhere, a mechanism for collecting debts, which can reduce households to income levels significantly below the poverty line.

A further issue that has aroused considerable concern — and that has been viewed as undermining the principle of parity — has been the higher cost of many basic necessities in Northern Ireland. The fact is that receipt of the same benefits does not secure the same standard of living for Northern Ireland's claimants. It is evident that basic necessities cost more than in Britain, that fuel costs are a particular problem and that an extraordinarily high proportion of the incomes of low income families is absorbed by a very limited range of essential expenses.[5]

In 1984, in evidence to the Assembly Health and Social Services Committee on Parity, many organisations concentrated on the issue of the cost of living in Northern Ireland. The question of price differentials is a difficult one, in that much of the data available (for example, from the Family Expenditure and Family Finances surveys) relate to what households actually spend — and this obviously depends on what they can afford, rather than what they need to spend to achieve a given standard of living. For this reason, though there are various drawbacks to the approach, many organisations relied for their evidence to the Committee on the Reward Regional Surveys (published every four months) which provide the only comprehensive source of information for comparing the cost of living in all UK regions. From this data, it was ed that — excluding housing costs — attaining any of the hypothetical standards of living used by Reward Regional vs costs more in Northern Ireland. On average, the difference between the cost of living in Northern Ireland and in the UK as a whole was about £400 a year.

More specifically, many groups stressed that the critical issue was the cost of key items within these overall standards; for these, the gap is wider. Thus, CPAG (NI) argued:

> We are concerned with the living standards of those at the bottom of our society and for these groups the cost of cut glass or private education is of no relevance at all. What matters is how do the costs of basic necessities compare. Social security benefits ought at least to enable all claimants, regardless of location, to purchase them. For this reason we would particularly direct the attention of the Committee to the cost of transport, food and fuel. In Northern Ireland, to reach an average standard of consumption of food, transport and fuel, one must spend £595 more than is required generally across the United Kingdom.[6]

The most recent assessment of the cost of living for low income households has been produced by Ditch and Wilson-Davies.[7] Based on Family Expenditure Survey and RPI data, their report reached three main conclusions. First, they confirmed that the cost of living is higher in Northern Ireland than in the rest of the UK. Second, they concluded that the cost of living for low income households in Northern Ireland is 5% higher than for other households in Northern Ireland. Finally, they suggested that the difference between the cost of living for those on low incomes in Northern Ireland and those on low incomes in Britain is of the order of 13%. In other words, the poorest region in the UK is the worst place to try living on the poverty line.

The issue of fuel costs has been at the centre of the cost of living debate and the discussion of parity. The first two reports of the Social Security Advisory Committee (SSAC) argued that parity in the limited sense of the word was acceptable, provided 'other factors bearing on the poorest groups in Northern Ireland and in Great Britain are kept in reasonable balance'.[8] SSAC clearly views fuel costs in Northern Ireland as upsetting the balance and rendering parity a facade. It concluded in its second report:

> The need for some further form of fuel cost relief for poor families in Northern Ireland over and above what is available to those experiencing similar problems in Great Britain seems to us both indisputable and urgent. If general help is not possible to reduce the tariff differential it may be necessary at some future date to reconsider the question of parity between the Great Britain and Northern Ireland social security systems in relation to the fuel costs of poor families.[9]

There are a number of reasons why low income households in

Northern Ireland, in particular, need a sensitive, coherent policy to tackle the problem of fuel poverty. In the 1970s, costs moved ahead of those in the UK. This occurred for two reasons: first, Northern Ireland did not gain access to North Sea gas, despite strong local representations on this issue; second, the sharp increases in oil prices had a deeper effect on electricity costs in Northern Ireland, as local power stations were more heavily dependent upon oil.

For a time, Northern Ireland claimants received higher heating additions under the SB scheme, and low income households generally were covered by a more generous fuel discount scheme. However, both measures were scrapped in 1980. Since 1981, the only concession by government has been to peg the cost of electricity for domestic consumers in Northern Ireland to the price paid in the most expensive region in Britain. Moreover, Northern Ireland's gas industry is currently being closed down, with the loss of 1,000 jobs, and the project to pipe gas from Kinsale has recently collapsed.

Table 2, which demonstrates the gap between costs in Northern Ireland and in Britain, shows that gas is much more expensive. Not surprisingly, few households depend on this form of heating. The result, as Table 3 indicates, is a much greater dependence amongst households in the poorest region of the UK — and the second poorest region in the EEC (after Calabria) — on what would, in Britain, be considered the more expensive forms of heating.

Table 2: *Fuel costs in Northern Ireland and Britain (1983)*

| Fuel | Pence per therm | | Pence per useful therm | |
	NI	GB	NI	GB
Oil	57.0	57.0	87.8	87.8
Coal	37.3	37.9	106.6	106.7
Gas	93.7	40.4	156.2	62.2
Electricity	186.7	170.2	207.5	189.1
Weighted average			138.8	101.2

Source: Assembly Report, Vol I, App VI, 1984

Table 3: *Market shares in Northern Ireland and Britain (1982)*

Fuel	NI	GB
Oil	19.7	6.3
Coal	42.4	10.4
Gas	4.1	57.6
Electricity	33.7	25.8

Source: Assembly Report, Vol I, App VI, 1984.

After reviewing all the evidence, the Assembly Committee on Social Security Parity concluded that in 1983, simply to obtain the same benefit, the average householder in Northern Ireland had to spend 40% more on fuel.[10] Whilst not wishing to overturn the general principle, the Committee argued that to secure parity in reality a fuel benefit of £3.50 per week should be paid to all claimants in receipt of housing benefit. To date, no action has been taken on this proposal.

The strain and lack of margin which these factors produce in household budgets was documented in the report of the Belfast Welfare Rights Project in 1980.[11] Just three items — food, fuel and housing — accounted for 75% plus of the actual incomes of the majority of those interviewed living around the poverty line, and nearly half of those interviewed faced weekly fuel costs amounting to more than 20% of their incomes. Supporting evidence for these data is to be found in the PPRU report,[12] which drew on information from the fuel questionnaire attached to Northern Ireland's Family Expenditure Survey (1980/82), Family Resources Survey (1980) and Household Finances Survey (1980/81). Table 4, reproduced from the report, indicates that nearly one-fifth of the incomes of low income families and nearly one-quarter of those of pensioners went on fuel.

Table 4: *Fuel expenditure as a proportion of net household income (%)*

	Low income families	*Low income pensioners*	*FES (all)*
Mean	17.1	24.2	14.1
Median	14.5	23.3	11.1

Source: J Mapstone, *Domestic fuel use and expenditure among low income groups*, PPRU 1984.

The PPRU report also demonstrated that fuel arrears are not randomly distributed across all types of household, at all income levels, with all types of heating — which is what one would expect if the problem of debt was due to mismanagement. Those in arrears tended to be families on low incomes who had to depend on electricity as the main source of heating. Most importantly, perhaps, the study concluded:

Low income households are not extravagant in their use of heating — households on supplementary benefit spend less on fuel than those not on supplementary benefit... Low income

11

groups spend less on fuel than other households of equivalent size... *There are no grounds for thinking that there is potential for reducing the level of heating in low income households or for suggesting that a reduction in heating might be a remedy for disproportionate fuel costs* (emphasis added).[13]

Conclusion

Whilst Northern Ireland's social security system is, in a crude sense, almost identical to that of Britain, there are differences in the administration of benefits, there is a much greater link between social security and debt collection, and, as a result of higher prices, parity in benefits has not meant the provision of a similar standard of living for claimants here.

References

1 For a fuller discussion, see D Birrell and A Murie, *Policy and Government in Northern Ireland: lessons of devolution*, London 1980.
2 *Northern Ireland Assembly Report: Social Security Parity*, Vol I, App 3, HMSO Belfast 1984.
3 For a fuller discussion see, for example, J Ditch, 'Social policy implications of emergency legislation in Northern Ireland', *Critical Social Policy*, Vol 1, no 3.
4 I am grateful to Les Allamby of the Belfast Law Centre for this information.
5 For further evidence of Northern Ireland's higher prices, etc, see E Evason, *Ends That Won't Meet*, CPAG 1980.
6 *Assembly Report*, Vol I, App VII.
7 J Ditch and K Wilson-Davis, *The cost of living for low income households in Northern Ireland*, Northern Ireland Consumer Council 1985.
8 *First Report of the Social Security Advisory Committee*, 1981, London HMSO, p 53.
9 *Second Report of the Social Security Advisory Committee*, 1982/3, London HMSO, p 54.
10 *Assembly Report*, Vol I, p 11.
11 E Evason, *Ends That Won't Meet*, CPAG 1980.
12 J Mapstone, *Domestic Fuel Use and Expenditure Among Low Income Groups*, Policy, Planning and Research Unit, Department of Finance and Personnel, Stormont 1984.
13 As note 11.

3 Dependence and key benefits

The distortions in parity outlined in the previous section are visited upon a population disproportionately liable to low incomes. As Table 5 indicates, whilst similar proportions of the populations of Britain and Northern Ireland are in receipt of the benefits listed, the claimant population in the former differs in composition from that of the latter. As a result of higher unemployment, and proportionately fewer people of retirement age, Northern Ireland's claimants are more dependent on the least adequate parts of the benefits system.

Table 5: *Distribution of claimant population across major benefits in Britain and Northern Ireland (1983)*

Benefit	% of claimant population in receipt of	
	NI	*GB*
Unemployment benefit	8.1	6.5
Sickness/invalidity benefit	11.4	8.2
Widows' benefits (excluding widow's allowance)	3.5	2.9
Retirement pension	49.6	66.7
Supplementary pension only	1.5	0.6
Supplementary allowance only	25.9	15.1
Total	*100.0*	*100.0*
Total claimants as % of total population	*25.2*	*25.4*

Sources: Social Security Statistics, London 1984, and *Northern Ireland Social Security Statistics*, Belfast 1984

The non-claimant population is also more at risk of poverty as a result of lower wages, the lower economic activity rate of women (only 41% of couples have two wages coming in, compared with 53% of couples on the mainland) and larger households.

The result is that, as Table 6 demonstrates, Northern Ireland households and individuals have the lowest weekly incomes in the UK, and a higher proportion of their incomes is made up of benefits. The local economy is, therefore, heavily dependent on the purchasing power provided by benefits and the prospect of further cuts is viewed with alarm.[1]

Table 6: *Weekly income, households and per person, 1982-3*

	Av no persons per household	Av weekly income per person	per household	% of households with less than £75pw	% of household income from benefits
United Kingdom	2.72	74.9	182.1	22.1	7.7
North	2.71	66.8	158.5	28.9	10.9
Yorkshire & Humberside	2.69	65.7	163.3	25.9	9.6
East Midlands	2.72	71.0	176.9	20.8	6.9
East Anglia	2.68	75.7	181.9	21.6	6.7
South East	2.67	89.4	210.5	17.0	5.2
South West	2.64	75.7	177.9	20.8	6.4
West Midlands	2.78	69.5	174.1	21.1	8.8
North West	2.73	69.2	174.1	24.9	9.1
England	2.70	76.7	185.4	21.3	7.2
Wales	2.75	64.6	166.4	21.9	10.6
Scotland	2.77	68.9	167.5	27.7	9.5
Northern Ireland	3.20	52.3	144.7	32.1	14.6

Source: Family Expenditure Surveys and Regional Statistics, 1985

Dependence on key means-tested benefits

The degree of dependence on certain benefits gives a guide to the total volume of poverty in Northern Ireland. It may, of course, be argued (as does the Green Paper) that there is no agreed definition of poverty or that, in any case, receipt of benefits indicates that the problem has been dealt with — albeit through dependence on means-tested aid. The first argument is undermined by the *Breadline Britain* survey,[2] which shows a considerable level of agreement across social classes on what constitutes the level of living below which individuals and families should not fall. The second argument is undermined by the considerable evidence, also supported by *Breadline Britain*, that, for families in particular, benefit levels are too low to cover the cost of what most would regard as essential items of expenditure. The latter point has (as is evident from the previous section on prices) particular significance in Northern Ireland.

(a) *Supplementary benefit*
As one would expect, Table 7 indicates that Northern Ireland's SB claimants are less likely than British claimants to be widows,

pensioners or single parents and more likely to be unemployed. This has a major and obvious significance, given that the unemployed are excluded from the higher long-term rate of benefit.

Table 7: *Composition of SB claimant population in Northern Ireland (1983) and Britain (1982) compared*

Category	NI	GB
Supplementary/pensioners	30.7	41.6
Unemployed	47.0	40.3
Sick/disabled	7.2	5.6
Widows/single parents	8.6	10.1
Others	6.2	2.1
Total	*100*	*100*

Sources: *Social Security Statistics*, London 1984, and *Northern Ireland Social Security Statistics*, Belfast 1985.

More broadly, as Table 8 indicates, in 1983, 22% of Northern Ireland's total population was wholly or partly supported by SB, compared with 13% in Britain in 1982. Moreover, in 1983, 24% of all Northern Ireland's children — nearly one-quarter — were in families dependent on SB, compared with 13% of all children in Britain. It can also be noted that nearly three-quarters of the children in Northern Ireland dependent on SB are in families pinned to the lower ordinary rate of benefit, and that these children account for one-sixth of the total child population in Northern Ireland. The exclusion of the unemployed from the long-term rate of benefits is, therefore, a major cause of child poverty in Northern Ireland.

Table 8: *Dependence on SB in Northern Ireland (1983) and Britain (1982)*

Dependence type	NI	GB
(a) % of total population dependent on SB	21.6	12.8
(b) % of total child population on SB	23.5	13.4
(c) % of children on SB in families of unemployed claimants	71.5	55.0
(d) (c) as % of total child population	16.8	7.4

Sources: *Social Security Statistics*, London 1984, and *Northern Ireland Social Security Statistics*, Belfast 1984

The latest information available (February 1985) suggests that 12% of the Northern Ireland population, leaving aside their dependants, are claimants of SB.

The greater poverty of Northern Ireland's claimants produced by this skewed distribution and other factors is demonstrated by two other characteristics of its SB claimants. First, they are less likely to have any savings to fall back on — in 1983, only 15.6% fell into this category, compared with 39.2% of British claimants (1982). Second, there is also a very high level of reliance on single payments, as Table 9 indicates. The most recent information available is that in the first six months of 1985, £13.7m was expended on single payments in Northern Ireland.

Table 9: *Single payments in Northern Ireland and other UK regions (1983)*

Region	Av payment £	No. per 1,000 live cases
Northern Ireland	113.14	720
Scotland	101.04	702
North Eastern	66.62	511
Midlands	70.67	379
London — North	83.95	254
— South	81.44	240
Wales and South West	66.31	378
North Western	65.15	484

Source: Northern Ireland Assembly Report: Social Security Parity, Belfast 1984

So, Northern Ireland's population is heavily dependent on SB; its SB claimants are poorer; nearly one child in every four is in a claimant family and one in six is in a family dependent on the lower ordinary rate of benefit. The likely cuts in general for many groups dependent on SB, and the cuts in single payments in particular, will have a severe impact on this region.

(b) *Family income supplement*

Some evidence of the level of need amongst the working poor — those who earn their poverty — is provided by the operation of family income supplement (FIS) (whilst bearing in mind, of course, that across the UK as a whole a significant proportion of those entitled fail to claim this benefit). Families in Northern Ireland are twice as likely to be on FIS as families in England, Scotland and Wales; the respective percentages being 6.1%, 2.7%, 3.3% and 3.7%

in 1983. Moreover, at least 7.8% of children (one in every 12) in Northern Ireland were in families dependent on FIS, compared with 3.2% of children in Britain. At the same time, as Table 10 indicates, FIS families are more likely to be two-parent (rather than single-parent) families — to a greater extent than elsewhere, the problem is one of low wages amongst men as well as women. In addition, Northern Ireland's FIS families on average have lower incomes, receive a higher amount of weekly benefit and are more likely to be on maximum awards.

Table 10: *FIS in Northern Ireland and Britain*

Indicator	NI (Oct '83)	GB (April '84)
% claims by 2-parent families	86.9	60.0
% claiming with total income £75.00+ pw	40.9	66.5
Average award	£15.96	£12.30
% claimants on maximum award	21.1	12.5

Sources: Social Security Statistics, London 1984, and *Northern Ireland Social Security Statistics*, Belfast 1984

More recent data, for June 1985, suggest that 6.8% of families in Northern Ireland are in receipt of this benefit. Here again, the Green Paper proposals and other indications of future policy have a particular significance for Northern Ireland. If the preferred model of family support for the future is to be credits, paid normally to husbands, with a declining role for child benefit, then across the UK the consequence will be greater financial dependence amongst women. For many women, child benefit is the only independent income they have and can control. For some, it is the only constant element in their weekly budgeting.[4] Married women in Northern Ireland are less likely to be in employment than elsewhere and are therefore particularly likely to have no other independent source of finance apart from child benefit.

(c) *Housing benefit*
In all, therefore, a quarter of the population of the region is supported by two key means-tested benefits. This is only a minimal estimate of poverty, however, and dependence on the third key benefit — housing benefit — suggests a very high level of need. Thus, for example, in July 1984, 69% of Executive tenants were in receipt of housing benefit and a further 9% were estimated to be entitled to, but not claiming, it. In total, in March 1985, 15% of

Northern Ireland's households were in receipt of standard housing benefit (ie, non-SB claimants); and if those on SB (26% of all households) are included, it would appear that at least two-fifths of the province's households could be said to be in low income households.[5]

References

1   See, for example, John Hume's speech in the House of Commons debate on Social Security (Reform), 18 June 1985.
2   S Lansley and J Mack, *Poor Britain*, London 1984.
3   See note 2 above and, for example, for Northern Ireland, E Evason, *Ends That Won't Meet*, CPAG 1980, and R Berthoud, *The Reform of Supplementary Benefit*, Policy Studies Institute 1984.
4   See A Walsh and R Lister, *Mother's life-line: a survey of how women use and value child benefit*, CPAG 1985.
5   D Graham, *The Cutting Edge*, North Belfast Community Resource Centre 1985

4 Groups at risk

(a) *The elderly*
There is a surprising absence of data on the circumstances of the elderly in Northern Ireland. Indeed, the last regional survey was in 1967. However, the information that is available is of interest here again, in that Northern Ireland may be viewed as an illustration of the potential weaknesses of the Green Paper's original proposals for pensions. The private pensions market does not beat a path to the doors of the low paid, unemployed or women engaged in socially necessary, but unpaid, work within the home. It can be argued that for such groups only state provision, with its capacity for crediting and redistribution, offers any prospect of pensions above the poverty line, and it seems likely that the region with more low pay, unemployment and female dependence than elsewhere has most to lose from any move towards privatisation.

Of Northern Ireland's population, 14.4% is of pensionable age, compared with 17.9% in Britain. Northern Ireland's very elderly population is also smaller, with 31% of the retired falling into the 75+ age group, compared with 34.4% of the elderly in Britain.

Increasing age is associated with greater poverty and it is therefore of interest that Northern Ireland's retired population, though younger, is more dependent on SB than that of Britain. At the end of 1983, 27% of the population of pensionable age was supported by the scheme, compared with 21.2% of the elderly in Britain.

Supplementary pensioners in Northern Ireland also appear to be poorer, with greater needs and more limited alternatives to state income. In 1983, 92.5% were in receipt of additions provided under the scheme for special expenses, compared with 91% of British supplementary pensioners; but the average addition was significantly higher, £4.47 compared with £3.15. Of Northern Ireland's additions, 57% were for heating, compared with 49.6% of additions paid to British supplementary pensioners — excluding the age-related provision.

Statistics for the same period also indicate that the majority (67.5%) of Northern Ireland's supplementary pensioners had no capital, compared with 41.3% of British pensioners, and, on a proportionate basis, nearly twice as many single payments to meet exceptional needs were made to Northern Ireland pensioner claimants as were paid in Britain. Moreover, the amounts paid were

19

on average more than double the payments made in Britain. Of particular current relevance is the fact that 18.1% of British supplementary pensioners had sources of income other than state benefits, compared with 10.8% of Northern Ireland's claimants. Most significantly, the bulk of the gap relates to receipt of superannuation payments — 13.7% of British supplementary pensioners had incomes from this source, compared with only 2.3% of Northern Ireland claimants.

This points to the much more general issue of pensions policy and the role of the private pensions sector in Northern Ireland. A central proposal of the Green Paper is the abolition of the state earnings related pension scheme and reliance on occupational pensions or personal pensions purchased in part with employers' contributions. The statistics in the Green Paper, however, deal almost exclusively with Britain. To overcome this problem, the DHSS (NI) produced a digest of statistical information,[1] but the most remarkable feature of this publication is, perhaps, the total absence of any information relating to membership of, or receipt of payments from, private occupational pension schemes. Hence, we are not given the most basic data necessary to facilitate an assessment of the effect of the government's proposals on Northern Ireland.

The data on supplementary pensioners does, however, suggest, as one would expect, that one result of the province's high unemployment and poorer quality employment is that the private pensions market has made a more limited contribution to bolstering the living standards of the elderly. Some support is given to this hypothesis by Inland Revenue data, which indicate that the population of Northern Ireland receives proportionately less from occupational pension schemes than any other region in the UK — and the differences appear marked, even allowing for differences in demographic structure, partly offset, in any case, by the fact that our pensioners are younger.

If the proposal to abolish SERPS goes ahead, much more regional analysis of its impact is clearly needed, and indeed such work ought to be undertaken by the government if it is to refute the argument that a policy which disadvantages entire regions makes little sense in terms of fairness or equity.

Finally, Graham's[2] work highlights the way in which pensioners in Northern Ireland, as in the UK as a whole, have been particularly affected by the introduction of housing benefit and subsequent cuts in the scheme. Exclusion of housing costs from assessment for SB entitlement meant that many pensioners were floated off the SB scheme. Housing benefit supplement — the price of a nil-cost housing benefit scheme — was designed to pick up and compensate those floated off. By early 1984, however, the number of claimants

Table 11: *Percentage of income from occupational pensions in all UK regions*

UK	3.6
North	3.2
Yorkshire & Humberside	3.1
East Midlands	3.1
East Anglia	5.1
South East	3.7
South West	5.2
West Midlands	2.8
North West	3.8
England	3.6
Wales	4.7
Scotland	3.5
Northern Ireland	2.5

Source: Central Statistical Office, *Regional Trends*, 1985

of housing benefit supplement — as a proportion of those floated off SB — was 64% in England and Wales, 75% in Scotland and 41% for Northern Ireland (January 1985). In other words, the mechanism intended to compensate pensioners removed from the SB scheme appears to have reached proportionately fewer such pensioners in Northern Ireland than elsewhere. Moreover, it has been estimated that the cuts in the scheme through increased tapers affected 24,000 standard housing benefit claimants in Northern Ireland — 36% of these being pensioners.

In summary, Northern Ireland's pensioners are poorer; their circumstances raise critical questions in relation to future pensions policy, and for this group the housing benefit scheme has been less than an advance.

(b) *Low income families*
In 1975, it was estimated that 30% of Northern Ireland's families lived below the level of income which gave entitlement to rent rebates at that time.[3] More recent data have been collected through the complex of surveys conducted by the PPRU of the Northern Ireland Department of Finance and Personnel. The Family Finances Survey (1978/9) for Northern Ireland followed closely the FFS for Britain, and concentrated on low income families identified by interviewing 2% of all families on child benefit.[4] These families were followed up one year later in the Family Resources Survey. Families that were identified as on the margins of poverty were also followed up in the Household Finances Survey. In addition, a school meals survey covered a sample of families identified in the

21

FFS exercise and was followed up by a survey of schoolchildren.[5] Not all of the data collected have been published.

The FFS interviews suggested that in Northern Ireland 29.5% of families were low income families — an estimate subsequently revised downward to 19.6%. The corresponding figures for Britain were 20.6% and 13%. Low income was defined in the conventional manner, used in the DHSS Low Income Family Tables, as the ordinary SB rate plus 40%.

The level of family poverty reported for 1978/9 appeared low at the time and would appear to be an uncertain base for estimates of family poverty in the 1980s. By 1983, 23% of families in Northern Ireland were on SB, and the majority of these were headed by unemployed persons on the ordinary rate — as were one-third of the non-unemployed claimants of supplementary allowances. In addition, receipt of the higher rate will, of course, normally be insufficient to raise families above the 140% level. To these families on SB must be added low income families dependent on other benefits and on low earnings. The data available are inadequate for the purpose of calculating the current volume of family poverty, but on this evidence an estimate of at least 35% plus living in poverty or on its margins (ie, ordinary SB rate plus 40%) would not appear unreasonable.

The FFS data remain, however, a useful frame of reference for comparison with Britain. They demonstrate that family poverty in Northern Ireland is associated with the same characteristics as family poverty in Britain — the problems are deeper but not fundamentally different. In both Northern Ireland and Great Britain, the majority of low income families in 1978/9 were those with four children or fewer — 82% of Northern Ireland's low income families fell into this category compared with 96% of British families. Amongst the two-parent families in Northern Ireland, 44% of those in poverty were headed by wage earners (Britain 60%) and 36% by unemployed persons (Britain 27%), with 12% of low income families being headed by sick or disabled persons (Britain 9%).

The school meals and schoolchildren's surveys are of interest for three reasons. First, they confirmed that the 1980 Act restricting free school meals to those on SB and FIS (only Belfast assists other low income families) cut the number of families entitled to aid by 40%. Second, the data undermined (as have numerous take-up campaigns since) the stereotype of Northern Ireland claimants knowledgeably applying for everything in sight. The take-up rate of free school meals was only 50%. Third, the survey of schoolchildren in families on or near the poverty line indicated that whilst they were not generally undernourished, their average protein intake fell below the levels advised by the DHSS for a well-balanced diet.

A further spin-off of the FFS was the production of data
presence of adult children in Northern Ireland households -
of FFS families were multi-unit households and Brads
analysis of their circumstances[6] highlights the need for more
mation about actual transfers of resources within households so
that policy can be based on empirical knowledge rather than
unrealistic assumptions.

To sum up, therefore, it appears that at least 35% of Northern
Irish families are in or on the margins of poverty, and that the
main causes are low wages and unemployment — not large families.
It is also evident that Northern Ireland has much to lose from
policies which cut the cost of the housing benefit scheme by
assuming ever larger contributions towards parental housing costs
from grown up children (regardless of their wage levels and the
quality of accommodation occupied).[7] Equally, policies which
off-load responsibility for the support of unemployed sons and
daughters from the state to parents, by cuts in the SB received by
young people living away from home as lodgers, or (if the Green
Paper's proposals for a lower benefit rate for under-25-year-olds
goes ahead) as householders, would hit very hard.

(c) Low pay

The prominence of low wages as a cause of family poverty in the
FFS and other data is hardly surprising. Northern Ireland has long
contained the highest concentration of low paid workers of any
UK region. Table 12 indicates that, in 1984, men in full-time work
in Northern Ireland had the lowest average weekly wage of any
UK region, despite being the most dependent on overtime. Nearly
one-quarter had gross earnings below £100 per week, which means
take home pay of £75-80 — roughly the equivalent of the long-term
SB rate for a married couple plus average housing costs of £16.

As in Britain, apart from FIS, the wages councils are the only
mechanism directly concerned with low paid workers. Northern
Ireland's councils can prescribe minimum wages, holidays and
holiday pay, but not, as Ditch and Steele note, other conditions of
employment.[8] Wages councils in Northern Ireland cover 8% of the
workforce and the wages set for a full week's work can hardly be
described as generous, ranging from £55.61 to £80.95.

The recent decision to exclude young people from the scope of
wages councils was strongly opposed by various groups in Northern
Ireland. On this issue, a recent survey of apprentice hairdressers in
Northern Ireland is instructive.[9] This is a case study of the consequences for young people who lack trade union protection and are
outside the scope of wages councils. Two-thirds of these young
people in Northern Ireland were earning less than the meagre £25
per week paid to those in the youth training programme. In

addition, only 10% had a contract of employment and only 47% had a recognised lunch break.

Table 12: *Male earnings in UK regions (1984)*

	Av weekly earnings £	Of which overtime pay £	% earning under £100 %
GB	178.8	14.7	12.6
North	167.5	14.1	13.6
Yorkshire & Humberside	167.4	15.1	14.5
East Midlands	164.6	15.0	14.3
East Anglia	166.9	15.2	15.7
South East	198.2	14.7	9.4
South West	166.1	13.8	16.0
West Midlands	167.0	14.1	12.7
North West	171.9	14.2	13.8
England	179.4	14.5	12.3
Wales	165.8	13.0	15.6
Scotland	178.7	16.5	13.8
Northern Ireland	164.1	17.9	24.0

Source: Regional Trends, London 1985

On the basis of Northern Ireland's experience, the view that there is widespread resistance to taking low paid jobs as benefits are too high is difficult to comprehend — as is the argument that more jobs will appear if wages and benefit levels are cut. A significant proportion of the labour force in Northern Ireland is, and always has been, employed on lower wages. Benefit levels have effectively been cut over the past few years, by higher prices, yet unemployment has soared and there is more competiton for fewer jobs than anywhere else. In 1982, for example, the ratio of unemployed persons to unfilled vacancies in Northern Ireland was 113:1 — more than twice the rate in the next worst-off region (the West Midlands), which had a ratio of 49:1.

(d) *Single-parent families*
The 1984 Continuous Household Survey for Northern Ireland indicated that single-parent families accounted for 11.4% of all families in Northern Ireland, compared with 13% in Britain (1981-83).

Single parents in Northern Ireland have faced special problems over the past 10 years. First, Northern Ireland's legislation relating to divorce and separation was only brought fully into line with

England and Wales in 1980. Second, services for the under-5s — of particular importance to single parents in employment or seeking work — lag far behind provision elsewhere. Northern Ireland's day nurseries were simply closed down at the end of the Second World War and to date, despite evidence of substantial need and demand for such provision, there is only one day nursery as such (excluding commercial ventures and facilities in the universities), and this is a voluntary effort.[10]

Data on the circumstances of single parents are provided by the FFS and a larger survey conducted in the same period which was published by the Northern Ireland Equal Opportunities Commission (NIEOC).[11] The FFS data indicated that, as in Britain, single parents were twice as likely to be in or on the margins of poverty as two-parent families, and low income single-parent families were twice as likely to be dependent on SB as low income two-parent families — reflecting the absence of non-means-tested provision for the bulk of single-parent families not in employment. The FFS categorised 39% of the 329 single-parent families in the general SIFT Survey as in or on the margins of poverty.

The NIEOC survey drew on samples of single parents from three benefit registers: widowed mother's allowance, SB and one-parent benefit. Six hundred and ninety-four single parents were interviewed: nearly 4% of all such families in Northern Ireland at that point in time. The data suggested that 68% of these families were in or on the margins of poverty. The survey also examined other aspects of the circumstances of single parents in Northern Ireland and underlined the importance of examining transfers within the family between husbands and wives. It is evident that policies which disregard this issue ignore an important aspect of poverty. In the NIEOC survey, significant numbers of separated and divorced women did not feel themselves to be poor as a result of single parenthood: they emphasised the advantages of a regular income under their control. The problem was that, for many women, 'single parenthood represented a movement from poverty as a result of the inequitable division in resources between husband and wife to poverty as a result of the lowness of benefits'.[12]

This is a critical issue in the current debate on the future of social security. Only 14% of female single parents in Northern Ireland reported that during their marriages family finances had been managed jointly, whilst 9% had had full control over family finances. What of the other 77%? Nearly half (34% of the total) reported receiving no support or support which was irregular and variable in amount. The remaining women received a fixed weekly amount for housekeeping and, of these, the report commented:

> The powerlessness of wives is evident from the frequency of
> spontaneous observations by significant numbers of single

parents that they had not known what the husband's wages were so had no idea of the family's total financial situation or that the allowance was inadequate and/or only a fraction of the husband's wages. Mrs X observed: 'I was supposed to do everything on £20 a week, but I think his wages were about £80.'[13]

The NIEOC survey highlighted the gap between the popular ideology of marriage as a partnership and the reality for many women of financial dependence, and the inadequacy of policies which treat the family as a unit within which it is assumed that resources are pooled and allocated rationally and fairly.

Leaving this issue aside, and taking all single parents together, it is clear from the survey that they face formidable problems. At the time of interview, the majority had no savings, nearly half reported shortages of essential clothing for themselves or their children, one-quarter appeared to be very socially isolated, and 17% reported three or more symptoms of depression. In addition, the survey indicated that the majority of single parents on benefit would have preferred to be in employment.

If one adds to all this the fact that half the separated and divorced women in the sample reported that violence had been a feature of their marriages,[14] it can be seen that, whilst single parents do not dominate the poverty population numerically, this sub-group requires special and extra consideration by virtue of the complex nature of their needs and circumstances.

In conclusion, the information on single parents for Northern Ireland highlights the inadequacies of proposals for a restructuring of the benefits system which reduces the income of many women. At the same time, it demonstrates that dependence on benefits is not the result of personal preference. The obstacles to work are lack of employment opportunities plus, in this case, lack of day-care facilities. Northern Ireland's single parents are disproportionately handicapped in relation to both factors and are thus more at risk of poverty.

(e) *Health*

Between 1978 and 1980, a 100% identification exercise of the handicapped and disabled in Northern Ireland was undertaken by an independent body. The final report concluded that the prevalence rate of handicap and disability was 3.5% of the population, and the central observation of the report was that:

While there are substantially fewer elderly people in proportion to the total population than in the rest of the UK, the prevalence rate of handicap is higher than reported for the UK for example by Amelia Harris. If the percentage of the population handicapped in each group were to be extrapolated back into the age

profile for the UK population, the percentage rate would tu.
out to be 3.86%, a figure well above most estimates of the
appreciably handicapped population of the UK as a whole.[15]

This paradox of a younger population with lower standards of
health has been evident for some time. Table 13 compares receipt
of benefits for the sick and disabled in Northern Ireland and Britain.

Table 13: *Sickness and disability benefits in Northern Ireland
and Britain (1983)*

% of population in receipt of	NI	GB
Attendance allowance	1.1	0.7
Mobility allowance	0.5	0.5
NCIP/HNCIP/invalidity benefit	2.8	1.7

Sources: Social Security Statistics, London 1984, and *Northern
Ireland Social Security Statistics*, Belfast 1984

With regard to health standards it should be noted that Northern
Ireland has long had the worst record of any UK region with regard
to stillbirths, perinatal mortality and infant mortality. Table 14
compares the position in 1983 in Northern Ireland with other
regions.

Table 14: *Still births, perinatal and infant mortality in all UK
regions*

	Still births*	Perinatal** mortality	Infant† mortality
United Kingdom	5.8	10.5	10.2
North	5.9	10.8	10.2
Yorkshire & Humberside	6.4	11.5	10.9
East Midlands	5.9	10.8	10.6
East Anglia	5.7	9.3	9.0
South East	5.3	9.4	9.2
South West	5.0	9.2	10.1
West Midlands	6.7	12.3	10.8
North West	5.6	10.6	10.6
England	5.7	10.3	10.0
Wales	6.0	11.3	10.7
Scotland	5.8	10.6	9.9
Northern Ireland	7.4	13.1	12.1

*   Rate per 1,000 live and still births
** Still births and deaths of children under 1 week per 100 live and still births
†   Deaths of infants under 1 year per 1,000 live births

Source: Regional Trends, London 1985.

ird report,[16] the poor record of Northern Ireland was ...ributed to lower incomes and poorer housing. On the ...it, it is worth noting that whilst significant progress was ...the 1970s, the latest data available (for 1984) indicate ...8% of dwellings in Northern Ireland are unfit and 15.4% in ...repairs costing more than £2,500 per dwelling.

...rly, many complex issues are involved in both receipt of benefits for sickness and disability and mortality rates; nevertheless, the data seem to reflect some of the costs of deprivation in Northern Ireland.

(f) *The unemployed*

In 1983, 80% of those questioned in the Continuous Household Survey rated unemployment as one of the most important problems facing the region. This is hardly surprising. The experience of the last five years has been traumatic, affecting both communities and devastating hitherto relatively prosperous areas.

The decline of Northern Ireland's traditional industries has been well documented; so also has the collapse of much of the new industry attracted in the 1960s and early 1970s by the most generous collection of incentives offered in any UK region. Northern Ireland was hit earlier and more deeply by the decline that has affected the bulk of regions in the UK, as much of the new industry that had developed was of precisely the kind that was to prove most vulnerable. For example, Northern Ireland attracted one-fifth of total UK employment in man-made fibres, and suffered commensurately when that sector collapsed generally. In addition, there have been some rather spectacular fiascos — notably the demise of the De Lorean car factory in West Belfast. It can be noted that Northern Ireland had high unemployment prior to the conflict — the 1978/9 economic collapse was not the product of it.

Table 15 illustrates the much sharper decline in manufacturing that has occurred in Northern Ireland by comparison with the UK as a whole. Second, it indicates that nearly half of those in work now are in public sector employment. Third, the figures give little support to the hopes pinned on the private services sector for bringing down unemployment — in a region where purchasing power is lower, this is perhaps hardly surprising.

Table 16 is of interest not because of the actual rates of unemployment but because of the points of similarity between the Northern Ireland profile and that of other regions in the UK.

As in other regions, the overall unemployment rate for Northern Ireland conceals considerable variations. Thus, in August 1985, the male unemployment rate for the province as a whole stood at 26.4%, but this figure concealed a range from 17.7% in Ballymena to 48.4% in Strabane.

28

Table 15: *Employment structure in Northern Ireland and the UK*

	Employees in employment as a percentage of total employment					
	1953		1974		1983	
	NI	UK	NI	UK	NI	UK
Primary	6.3	8.4	2.2	3.3	2.0	3.1
Manufacturing	45.1	39.8	34.6	34.6	22.0	26.6
Construction	7.6	6.4	7.9	5.8	5.4	4.8
Private services	27.6	31.1	20.2	25.9	24.9	33.0
Public services	13.4	14.4	35.1	30.3	45.7	32.5

Source: B Black, 'Regional trade union growth', Queens University, Belfast

Table 16: *Unemployment by region 1976, 1980, 1984*

	Unemployment rate			% male unemployed 1 yr+
	1976	1980	1984	1984
United Kingdom	5.5	6.8	13.3	44.2
North	7.2	10.4	18.8	47.5
Yorkshire & Humberside	5.3	7.3	14.8	43.7
East Midlands	4.5	6.1	12.5	42.1
East Anglia	4.7	5.3	10.1	36.9
South East	4.0	4.2	9.7	38.3
South West	6.2	6.4	11.7	35.9
West Midlands	5.5	7.3	15.7	50.8
North West	6.7	8.5	16.1	48.9
England	5.1	6.4	12.8	43.6
Wales	7.1	9.4	16.8	44.6
Scotland	6.7	9.1	15.2	44.1
Northern Ireland	9.5	12.8	21.0	55.8

Source: Regional Trends, 1985

Table 17 demonstrates the irrelevance of unemployment benefit in maintaining the incomes of the unemployed across the UK generally, and particularly in Northern Ireland, where three-quarters of the unemployed on benefit were only entitled to means-tested supplementary allowances in 1983.

The impact of unemployment on the Northern Ireland SB scheme has, as elsewhere, been dramatic. Between 1979 and 1983, the number of unemployed claimants increased by 157%, and the unemployed accounted for the bulk (83%) of the 51% increase in the total number of persons claiming benefit in that period. In addition, by 1983, nearly one-third (31.5%) of unemployed SB claimants had been on benefit for more than two years.

Table 17: *Unemployed claimants by benefit entitlement (1983)*

Region	Unemployment benefit payable (%)		Supplementary allowance only (%)	
	Males	Females	Males	Females
GB	29.2	36.4	60.0	44.9
England	29.1	36.2	59.6	44.9
South East	30.4	36.9	56.5	44.0
East Anglia	32.0	40.9	54.0	40.9
South West	31.4	39.3	53.7	39.3
West Midlands	25.4	31.9	64.5	47.4
East Midlands	31.9	39.2	56.5	41.1
Yorkshire & Humberside	29.4	36.2	59.8	47.5
North West	26.7	34.9	63.8	46.3
North	30.0	34.4	60.0	47.5
Wales	29.0	34.0	62.3	46.8
Scotland	29.9	39.2	62.1	44.1
Northern Ireland	22.5	37.7	74.6	50.5

Source: Regional Trends, 1985

Apart from such purely statistical information, the data accumulated over the past 10 years have focused mainly on the differences between the two communities in Northern Ireland with regard to the risk of unemployment and, by implication, of poverty. The 1971 census had indicated that Catholics accounted for two-thirds of the unemployed, although they constituted only one-third of the population. Throughout the 1970s, substantial effort was expended on assessing the causes of this discrepancy.

The re-analysis of the 1976 government Cohort Survey of the unemployed by Miller and Osborne[17] reached a number of conclusions. First, there was a basic similarity between the Catholic and Protestant unemployed with regard to variables such as skill levels, education, concern about being out of work and so on. Nevertheless, there were significant differences, to the disadvantage of Catholics, with regard to frequency and duration of unemployment and age when first registering as unemployed.

These differences could, of course, be attributed to historical factors not yet having worked themselves out of the employment structure. For this reason, the 1977-8 survey of boys entering the labour force in Belfast, Derry and Strabane is of interest. In Belfast, for example, little difference was found between the two groups with regard to educational attainment, but only 37.2% of Catholics had found jobs within eight months of leaving school, compared with 60.8% of Protestants. It was noted that the major method of recruitment was informal recommendations and the authors concluded:

> We found a remarkable degree of openness in the areas in which boys suggested they would be willing to work. Hence, a major conclusion of the study is that those who exhort the unemployed, particularly in areas like Catholic West Belfast, to be more prepared to move to find work should perhaps spend an equivalent time persuading employers to institute recruiting procedures which take account of this potential mobility of labour.[18]

Also in the 1970s, Miller's research suggested little difference between the two communities with regard to attitudes to work.[19] The situation continues into the 1980s, with the most recent data, for 1983/4, indicating that Catholics are twice as likely to be unemployed as Protestants.[20]

In the 1980s, two studies have focused on the impact on the individual of unemployment, regardless of religion. Marshall's work demonstrated that unemployment is strongly associated with low mental health.[21] Trew and Kirkpatrick have examined the life styles of the unemployed in Belfast and compared their results with those of Miles for Brighton.[22] The Belfast survey of 136 unemployed men — half Protestant and half Catholic — indicated that only 12 felt unemployment had made no change in their lives, while the rest reported overwhelming negative changes — notably lack of money, boredom and poorer mental and physical health. With regard to measured psychological well-being, 64% of these Belfast men scored above the threshold recommended by Goldberg and 'could be described as having a tendency to minor psychiatric disorder'.

When compared with the Brighton unemployed, a remarkable similarity in life style emerged. The Belfast unemployed had not evolved different ways of coping on a day-to-day basis with unemployment. There were no significant differences between the two groups with regard to their perception of the impact of unemployment on their physical health, though the Brighton sample were in poorer health psychologically. It is clear, however, that the experience of worklessness is not dramatically affected by residence in an area with ample experience of unemployment. The authors note:

31

Despite extreme environmental differences, similarities in patterns of behaviour and the relation of these patterns to mental health among unemployed men were clearly apparent. These results perhaps indicate identifiable patterns of behaviour nationwide with such pattenrs being consistently related to mental health in stressful situations.

Thus, the evidence available on unemployment in Northern Ireland indicates that the province has long had the worst unemployment problem of any UK region, and that the burden of this problem is carried to a disproportionate extent by the minority community. In the light of this, it is perhaps surprising that there has been so little research focusing squarely on the issue of deprivation amongst the unemployed and their families in Northern Ireland as a whole. It is also noteworthy that virtually nothing has been produced on the deprivation amongst the unemployed in Derry — Northern Ireland's second largest city — with its long history of poverty and worklessness. Nor are there any available data comparing the circumstances of the unemployed in the two communities. These gaps were the starting point for the research project reported in the second half of this pamphlet. In effect, the intention was to survey the needs of the poorest of the poor within Northern Ireland.

References

1 *Northern Ireland Digest of Statistical Information Relating to Review of Social Security*, Central Review Unit, DHSS, Stormont, 1985.
2 D Graham, *The Cutting Edge*, North Belfast Community Resource Centre 1985.
3 E Evason, *Family Poverty in Northern Ireland*, CPAG 1978.
4 J Graham, *Family Finances Survey (VI)*, Occasional Papers, Policy Planning and Research Unit, Dept of Finance and Personnel, Stormont, 1983.
5 *School meals survey report*, PPRU 1982, and *Schoolchildren survey*, PPRU 1983.
6 J Bradshaw, *Families Sharing Poverty*, PPRU Occasional Paper 6.
7 As note 5 above.
8 J Ditch and R Steele, 'Minimum wage legislation in Northern Ireland', *Administration*, Vol 3, no 3.
9 L Egerton, *Apprentice Hairdressers in Northern Ireland*, Women's Centre, 16-18 Donegall Street, Belfast, 1984.
10 For a fuller discussion see, for example, E Evason, *Who Needs Day Care: a study of provision for the under-5s in Northern Ireland*, NI Equal Opportunities Commission 1982.
11 E Evason, *Just Me and the Kids*, NIEOC 1981.
12 As note 11 above, p 22.
13 As note 11 above, p 73.
14 See E Evason, *Hidden Violence*, Farsett Press 1982.
15 *'Action on Handicap' Survey in Northern Ireland, Final Report*, Outset, London, 1983.
16 Report of the Advisory Committee on Infant Mortality and Handicap in

Northern Ireland, *You and Your Baby*, Belfast 1980.

17 In R Cormack and R Osborne (eds), *Religion, Education and Employment*, Appletree Press 1983, Ch 5.

18 As note 17 above, p 160.

19 R Miller, *Attitudes to Work in Northern Ireland*, Fair Employment Agency, Belfast, 1978.

20 PPRU, 'Continuous Household Survey', *Monitor*, February 1985.

21 R Marshall, 'The psychological effects of unemployment on men with dependent children', unpublished MSc thesis, Queen's University, Belfast.

22 K Trew and R Kilpatrick, *The Daily Life of the Unemployed*, Dept of Psychology, Queen's University, Belfast, 1984.

The Derry survey: background

The city of Derry is located in the far north west of the province, close to the border with the Republic. Technically, the city's name is Londonderry, but to the majority of people in the area it is Derry. The city has a population of roughly 83,000 people and straddles the river Foyle. The city centre inside the old walls of Derry is tiny and scarred by bombing. Apart from the city centre and a handful of streets, some very fine, of private residential accommodation, Derry consists of large housing estates encircling the city and sprawling out in all directions.

Derry has its own culture and history. It is only 75 miles to Belfast, but the two cities are separated by more than the Glenshane Pass. The culture is a mixture of humour, pride, doggedness and bitterness; there is an assumption that little should be expected, for less will be given. The history is one of conflict, shirt factories and deprivation. The majority of the population is Catholic, but until the reforms of the late 1960s, the Unionist party had controlled the council for nearly half a century. There are records of extreme deprivation and suffering in the 1930s — which were largely ignored.[1] In the 1960s, the city was angered by the decision to locate the province's second university in Coleraine rather than in Derry. Derry is the city of the Battle of the Bogside and Bloody Sunday. More recently, supergrass trials have had a deep and corrosive effect on the community. Violence is never far away. Troops and police are regularly shot at and petrol-bombed.

In some ways, things have improved over the past decade or so. The slums of the Bogside have been cleared and some of the most recent housing schemes are as pleasant as can be found anywhere in the UK. The environment is, in some respects, better; but unemployment — the key problem in Derry — remains. In August 1985, the male unemployment rate was 38.5%. It has always been high, and unemployment has a central place in the culture of Derry: the songs, the writing and the jokes. It is an article of faith that the history of Derry is a history of husbands on the dole and wives in the shirt factories. This view of history may not be accurate, but it is what people believe.

Research in the mid-1970s suggested that the worst concentration of child poverty in Northern Ireland was to be found in Derry,[2] but apart from this one passing reference to the city, it is difficult to find any other data on poverty in Northern Ireland's second city. There is no material corresponding to the BAN (Belfast Areas of Special Need) Report and subsequent surveys which charted the spatial distribution of poverty in Belfast.[3] Northern Ireland's equivalent of the urban aid programme was in response to the BAN report, and hence confined to Belfast. The need in Belfast is obvious, but Northern Ireland has lacked a province-wide strategy which would have encompassed other areas, and Derry in particular.

In an attempt to fill some of the gaps in information, CPAG (NI) decided in 1983 to conduct a survey in Derry to examine the circumstances and attitudes of the unemployed and, in particular, those of the long-term unemployed. The decision to undertake the research was based on three grounds. First, there was a surprising lack of information focusing purely on poverty amongst the unemployed in Northern Ireland as a whole, and virtually no information was available for Derry — a city with a long tradition of high unemployment. Second, across Britain, the unemployed are the subject of negative, denigrating stereotypes and assumptions — and the position would appear to be little different in Northern Ireland. It was, therefore, felt that evidence gathered locally would be of assistance to CPAG (NI) in responding to these stereotypes and assumptions. Third, CPAG (NI) was interested in comparing the impact of unemployment on individuals and families from the two communities with a view to facilitating more adequate assessment of locally-bred stereotypes and assumptions.

More broadly, there was concern that across the UK the concept of full employment as a proper and central objective of social and economic policy was being abandoned, and that this would be followed by rationalisations to the effect that such a deep-rooted change was feasible and justifiable as individuals and families could, and would, adjust to unemployment. Indeed, the observation that unemployment is less of a problem in a city such as Derry, as 'they are used to it', has been current for some time. Developing out of this, it was felt that if anyone had had ample opportunity to discover methods of surviving unemployment, it was the people of Derry. Conversely, if those subject to worklessness in such as area have still not evolved coping mechanisms, then there is little prospect or hope for those in other UK regions — and there can be no fudging of the consequences of retreating from the goal of full employment.

Accordingly, a questionnaire was drawn up by CPAG (NI) and a research assistant recruited. In 1983, 264 unemployed male household heads were identified and interviewed through a house-to-house exercise conducted in a predominantly Catholic area. This constituted the 1st sample. In 1984, resources became available to supplement this effort with a 2nd sample, and a further 79

Interviews were completed in a predominantly Protestant area. The questionnaire focused on the living standards of the unemployed and their families; perceptions of self, attitudes and life styles of the unemployed; unemployment across generations; and some aspects of the benefits system.

References

1 See, for example, E Evason et al, *Social need and social provision in Northern Ireland*, Occasional Papers in Social Administration, New University of Ulster 1976.
2 E Evason, *Family Poverty in Northern Ireland*, CPAG 1978.
3 *Belfast: Areas of Special Social Need*, Report by Project Team, Belfast 1976, and, for example, *Belfast Household Survey*, Northern Ireland Housing Executive, Belfast 1978.

6 General characteristics

In both the 1st and 2nd sample the interviews were normally conducted with both husbands and wives — 95% in the 1st sample and 96% in the 2nd. Table 18 indicates that those interviewed fell into a limited range of household types and were predominantly two-parent families with dependent children. Families in the 2nd sample were, however, less likely to have non-dependent children and were younger families.

Table 18: *Household type (%)*

Household type	1st sample	2nd sample
2 parents + dependent children	70.4	75.9
2 parents + dependent and non-dependent children	20.4	13.9
Male single parent with dependent children	1.5	1.3
Other*	7.6	8.9

* Eg, single men, widowers with non-dependent children

Tables 19 and 20 indicate that male and female household heads in the 1st sample were slightly older than those in the second. In both samples, the majority of these unemployed men were under 45.

Table 19: *Age distribution of male household heads (%)*

Age	1st sample	2nd sample
Under 25	11.6	18.1
25—34	32.2	28.6
35—44	35.7	35.1
45—54	15.5	15.6
55+	5.0	2.6

Table 20: *Age of female household heads (%)*

Age	1st sample	2nd sample
Under 25	15.6	20.8
25—34	37.9	31.9
35—44	30.1	31.9
45—54	12.1	12.5
55+	4.3	2.8

Table 21 indicates that whilst the families in the 1st sample were twice as likely to have more than five dependent children, nevertheless in both samples large families were in the minority.

Table 21: *Number of dependent children (%)*

Dependent children	1st sample	2nd sample
0	7.2	10.1
1/2	32.6	45.5
3/4	41.7	34.2
5/6	14.4	8.9
6+	4.1	1.3

Table 22 relates to an important theme dealt with in the first section of this pamphlet, for it shows that in both the 1st and 2nd samples significant numbers of households contained non-dependent children — the figures being one-quarter and one-fifth respectively.

Table 22: *Non-dependent children (%)*

Non-dependent children	1st sample	2nd sample
0	74.6	79.7
1	11.0	8.9
2	6.4	3.8
3+	8.0	7.6

To sum up, we interviewed 343 households — the largest effort to date of this kind in Northern Ireland. Of these, 22% were from a predominantly Protestant area. The majority were families with dependent children and in both samples large families were in the minority. The 2nd sample consisted of slightly younger families, but both groups contained a significant number of households with grown-up non-dependent children.

7 Unemployment: past, present and future

The depth of unemployment in these communities was charted by reference to the experience of those interviewed and also that of their parents and their own children.

Table 23 demonstrates that, for those interviewed, unemployment normally meant long-term unemployment. In both samples, more than two-thirds of these men had been out of work for more than two years. There is, however, a slightly greater concentration of long-term unemployment among the 1st sample. One possible explanation for this relates to the difference in age between these two sets of unemployed men, but even when this was taken into account a gap remained. Thus, 71.4% of men under 40 in the 1st sample had been unemployed for more than two years, compared with 61.5% of men in the same age group in the 2nd sample.

Table 23: *Duration of unemployment (%)*

Duration of unemployment	1st sample	2nd sample
Less than 6 months	3.0	5.0
6 months — under 1 year	11.0	8.9
1 year — under 2 years	12.2	19.0
2 years — under 5 years	33.8	40.5
5 years +	40.0	26.6

For these families, unemployment reached forward and back. The 1st sample households contained 150 non-dependent children, and only 40% of these were in employment — 38% were unemployed, and the remainder were in higher education or youth schemes. The 2nd sample contained 30 non-dependent children and 16 of these were out of work at the time of the interview.

Thus, in both communities, for a significant proportion of parents with grown-up children the fact that their children had left school simply meant the addition of one more unemployed person to the household. The hard reality which must be faced by those who promote policies which cut benefit levels for young people and assume that parents can take more and more of the strain is that such young people are likely to be disproportionately concentrated amongst families that are already hard-pressed.

It was noted that in Derry it is firmly believed that the past is about workless men and working mothers. The survey data, which are supported by unpublished evidence,[1] suggest that this is a myth. Husbands and wives in both samples were asked about their recollections of the employment patterns of their own parents. The results are surprising and, perhaps, important. For a community to have a depressed perception of itself is bad enough, but the position is worse if that perception is based on folk lore that is inaccurate. If our data are correct, the reasons for the persistence of this Derry mythology deserve further investigation, in view of its impact on expectations, relationships between men and women, and the self-confidence of the whole community.

Tables 24 and 25 indicate that, whilst in both samples a significant number of husbands and wives came from families where the father was normally unemployed or 'in and out of work', the majority did not. The experiences of the two communities differ, but they are not poles apart. Nevertheless, the record of the past is bad enough in the sense that these couples grew up in the late 1940s and 1950s, when much of the rest of the UK had a labour shortage.

Table 24: *Employment patterns of fathers of male household heads (%)*

	1st sample	2nd sample
Mainly in full-time employment	65.4	79.8
Occasional spells of unemployment	10.9	7.6
Out of work more often than in work	3.9	2.5
Normally unemployed	19.8	10.1

Table 25: *Employment patterns of fathers of female household heads (%)*

	1st sample	2nd sample
Mainly in full-time employment	67.5	86.7
Occasional spells of unemployment	8.8	4.0
Out of work more often than in work	5.2	2.7
Normally unemployed	18.5	6.6

Tables 26 and 27 also suggest that some adjustment of popular perceptions of past family life may be required, for in both samples working mothers had been in the minority. Table 28 indicates that in both samples, the majority of men had lost their jobs through closure and redundancy; a minority had lost their employment

40

through sickness and had never been able to get back into employment; and a handful had simply never worked.

Table 26: *Employment patterns of mothers of male household heads (%)*

	1st sample	2nd sample
Normally in full-time work	21.3	16.9
Normally in part-time work	5.0	7.8
Normally full-time work with spells of unemployment	1.2	—
Full-time home care	72.5	75.3

Table 27: *Employment patterns of mothers of female household heads (%)*

	1st sample	2nd sample
Normally in full-time work	12.7	24.0
Normally in part-time work	4.8	13.3
Normally full-time work with spells of unemployment	—	—
Full-time home care	82.5	62.7

Table 28: *Causes of unemployment (%)*

	1st sample	2nd sample
Closure/redundancy	69.3	61.5
Health	13.8	14.1
Never worked	1.9	1.3
Other	15.0	23.1

Thus, in both samples, unemployment meant worklessness extending over years rather than months. For some, it was a repeat experience of what their fathers had lived through and, for many, their children were moving into the same pattern of life. Closures and redundancies were the main causes of lost jobs.

It is of interest, however, that the survey does not support local perceptions of the past, and whilst there is a difference between the two communities, this is less wide than might have been expected. With regard to the future, the prospects for the children of the unemployed of both samples appear bleak.

Reference
1   E McGlaughlin, World Development Group, Derry, unpublished data.

8 Living standards: past and present

(a) *Assessed impact of unemployment*

One of the obvious elements in the lives of these households was financial pressure. Their experience disproves any notion that in some way Northern Ireland's households have adjusted to unemployment and, in particular, learned ways of coping on poverty line incomes.

All of these households had incomes less than 10% above the poverty line and 92% were on SB. Many of them appeared to be in a state of total financial chaos, but the majority reported that life had not always been like this. In both samples, the majority (62% and 81%) reported that their incomes whilst employed had been adequate or better for meeting their needs — 14% of the 1st sample had been in receipt of means-tested aid while working, compared with 6% of the 2nd sample.

Not surprisingly, therefore, the majority in both samples reported that unemployment made a great difference to their standard of living.

Table 29: *Impact of unemployment on living standards (%)*

	1st sample	2nd sample
No difference	8.8	2.5
Some difference — worse	10.7	11.4
A lot of difference — worse off	63.2	77.2
Difficult to say as so long since employed	15.3	7.6
Better off	2.0	1.3

An open-ended question on the most noticeable difference made to living standards brought predictable responses: greater difficulty in paying fuel bills, problems replacing furniture and 'just budgeting each week'. Again, interviewees in both samples made similar responses, though again the 2nd sample appeared to be in more difficulty.

Table 30: *Households reporting various effects of unemployment (%)*

	1st sample	2nd sample
Difficulty paying fuel bills	64.5	88.6
Budgeting generally	60.3	84.6
Replacing furniture	60.3	83.5
Other	8.0	3.8

(b) *Current living standards and costs*

Fifteen indicators were used to assess current living standards, and Table 31 presents basic data in relation to these. The items listed, apart from possession of a car and phone, are generally in line with those that, according to the *Breadline Britain* survey,[1] the majority of people regard as essential. Taking the data as a whole, it appears that households in the 2nd sample are consistently in greater difficulty than those in the 1st — a finding which again undermines some of the cultural stereotypes of Northern Ireland.

Looking at each indicator more closely, it is noticeable that very few households have any margin in their weekly resources to provide for future needs or emergencies. In a supplementary question, interviewees were asked if they had actually had an unexpected call on their resources recently which had posed a problem: 48% of households in the 1st sample and 43% in the 2nd reported that they had. These households' definition of 'emergency', however, was of interest. For low income families, an 'emergency' is often what the more affluent might regard as normal, predictable expenditure. For these households, a financial catastrophe was receipt of the quarterly electricity bill or the new clothing needed at the start of the school year. It is also noticeable that some of these items were those for which single payments might have been claimed, while others illustrate gaps in provision — most obviously, assistance with the cost of school uniforms for primary school children, which is not available in Northern Ireland.

'The death of my mother. We had to help with expenses of £300 and got a credit union loan.'

I had a miscarriage and there was expenditure on clothing. We had to borrow from a relative.'

'We needed shoes for the children — £72.'

'The children going back to school and needing primary school uniforms, they cost £120.'

'The children starting back at grammar school — the problem of fees for books £34.'

'The washing machine needed a repair. It was £55. I'm trying to arrange to pay fortnightly.'

'We had to fix the fridge — £60.'

'We had to repair a faulty fire — it cost £80.'

'The last electricity bill — £120.'

Table 31: *Indicators of living standards (%)*

	1st sample	2nd sample
Unable to put money aside for emergencies	94	95
Borrows regularly	81	87
Unable to afford Christmas presents for children	23	31
Never purchases butter	23	55
Never purchases fresh meat (other than mince)	11	27
Female household head regularly goes without main meal	36	57
Adults in household lacking essential items of clothing	68	79
Children in household lacking essential items of clothing	64	76
Most recent purchase of new clothing male or female head of household more than 1 year prior to interview	45	68
Has not had a family holiday in previous 12 months	88	91
Possession of consumer goods		
does not have fridge	9	6
does not have telephone	61	87
does not have washing machine	11	20
does not have vacuum cleaner	15	22
does not have car	86	97

Table 31 also shows that in both samples the majority of households were borrowing regularly. Across both communities, a remarkable juggling act was being performed, with small amounts of money being pushed around the neighbourhood. Normal sources of credit played only a limited role in this process: 18% of households in the 1st sample and 8% in the 2nd relied in the main on the local credit union, but generally households depended on relatives and neighbours.

'We borrow from the credit union when clothing is needed.'

'We go to relatives for dinner when we cannot afford to eat.'

'I feel ashamed that I had to borrow from my 84-year-old mother who is getting the pension.'

The need to borrow also emerged in connection with children's Christmas presents. In both samples, significant minorities of parents had been unable to buy these at all — relatives, particularly grandparents, had filled the gap. Those parents who had bought presents divided up fairly evenly between those parents who had used catalogues, those who had borrowed the money and those who had cut down on other essential items of expenditure, for example, food.

'We had to go into debt. You're paying from one Christmas to the next.'

'We had to miss three weeks' rent in order to buy presents.'

'We get them with the help of a catalogue.'

The choice of food as an indicator of living standards presents problems — more research on what food is considered customary and essential is needed generally in Ireland. The consumption of butter and fresh meat may, however, have a particular cultural significance here, and these items had simply been cut out of the diets of significant numbers of households interviewed — with, once again, the 2nd sample more likely to be going without. In addition, the extra strain borne by women is evident from Table 31, with over one-third of the women in the 1st sample and more than half of those in the 2nd reporting that they regularly did without at least one main meal during the day.

Although a difference between the 1st and 2nd samples is also evident with regard to essential clothing (for example, winter coats), there were shortages across the board — in particular, high proportions of both husbands and wives had not purchased a single new item of clothing or footwear for themselves over the previous year.

Lastly, Table 31 indicates that the majority of households had three of the more basic consumer goods listed, but only a minority in both samples had been able to afford a holiday in the previous 12 months.

If the ownership of consumer goods is excluded from the analysis, we are left with 10 indicators of poverty. Table 32 indicates that using the fairly stringent cut-off point of being in difficulty over five or more items, nearly half of the 1st sample (49%) and four-fifths (81%) of the 2nd could be described as very hard-pressed. (Further analysis indicated that the difference is not the result of larger families or a longer period out of work.) Once again, we can only hypothesise that this is a cultural difference, but if the 1st sample are considered to be the more 'capable' households, this hardly adds up to managing well.

Table 32: *Scores on 10 indicators (%)*

Score	1st sample	2nd sample
0	0.8	—
1	6.1	1.3
2	12.1	—
3	16.3	6.3
4	15.9	11.4
5	26.5	19.0
6	12.9	21.5
7	6.4	19.0
8	3.0	19.0
9	—	2.5
10	—	—

Finally, as part of this section of the interview, households were asked about the method of transport they used to go into the city centre. The answers revealed more about the isolation of these households than their means of getting about. In both samples, many (49% 1st sample, 50% 2nd sample) simply didn't go into the centre. Those who did relied mainly on public transport.

(c) *Current costs*
That households should be as hard-pressed as this is hardly surprising in the light of the actual costs they faced. Table 33 indicates that, as one would expect from the evidence cited earlier, just one item (fuel) was absorbing more that one-fifth of the weekly incomes of the majority of households in both samples.

Table 33: *Weekly heating costs as a % of total weekly income*

% of income	1st sample	2nd sample
— 10%	7.9	11.4
10—19%	32.8	31.6
20—29%	33.2	34.2
30—34%	18.2	12.6
35% +	7.9	10.2

The lack of room for manoeuvre in weekly budgets, which produces shortages, borrowing and debt, is evident in Table 34. In

Table 34: *Housing, heating and food costs as % of total weekly income*

% of income	1st sample	2nd sample
− 50%	0.4	1.3
50—59%	0.4	3.8
60—69%	2.9	8.9
70—79%	13.6	21.5
80—89%	81.1	62.0
90% +	1.6	2.5

both samples, just three items (housing and heating costs and food expenditure) accounted for over 70% of the incomes of the majority of households.

(d) *Debt*

In Northern Ireland there is still an undertone to the debate on debt to the effect that, to a significant extent, it is a product of an irresponsible refusal to pay one's way, and that this attitude is particularly prevalent in the minority community. To compound this, the Fowler review proposes to replace single payments with a social fund, which would assist families in difficulty largely through advice on budgeting and loans.

Our information undermines these propositions and proposals. First, wilful refusal to pay hardly squares with the anxiety and worry about debt noted below. Second, debt was a problem for significant numbers of households in both samples. Third, can DHSS officers really find a way to help families to live on what is left of their benefits after deductions for loans, which would be piled on top of fuel direct, deductions under the Payments for Debt Act, HP and clothing cheque commitments? Table 35 shows that the majority of households were in debt.

Table 35: *The extent of debt*

Debt type	1st sample	2nd sample
% households in debt of any kind	77.7	86.1
% households reporting rent arrears	34.6	35.4
% households reporting electricity arrears	29.2	30.3
% households with other fuel debts	1.2	5.1
% households with HP commitments	35.4	32.9
% households with clothing cheque payments	35.6	40.5

With regard to rent arrears, the majority of households in both samples (72% and 63% respectively) reported that the amounts owed were in excess of £100. For electricity arrears, 61% of those in debt in 1st sample households and 58% in the 2nd sample owed £150 plus. In both samples, less than one-third of households had no such debts or commitments (19.9% and 29.1%); more than half (54% 1st sample, 52% 2nd sample) had one or two such debts; whilst 16% of the 1st sample and 19% of the 2nd had three or four.

Table 36 suggests that debt is related to the presence and number of dependent children

Table 36: *Rent and electricity arrears by number of dependent children*

Arrears type		No of children		
		0	1-2	3+
% with rent arrears	1st sample	21.0	29.1	38.4
	2nd sample	25.0	36.1	41.9
% with electricity arrears	1st sample	15.8	29.1	30.1
	2nd sample	25.0	27.8	34.3

A separate paper is being prepared on debt (to be published in 1985); but the data presented here underline again the importance of proposals for change taking account of the reality and dynamics of the financial circumstances of low income households.

Summary

In conclusion, it would appear that for the great majority of these households unemployment meant a lower standard of living. The majority could not save for emergencies and were borrowing regularly. In both samples, the majority of those interviewed reported shortages of essential clothing and, on the 10 indicators of need used, half of the 1st sample and 81% of the 2nd could be described as very hard-pressed. In the light of actual expenditure on food and fuel and housing costs, this lack of room for manoeuvre was predictable. Finally, the majority of households in both samples had debts of one kind or another.

Reference
1   J Mack and S Lansley, *Poor Britain*, London 1984.

9 Some other consequences of unemployment

This part of the questionnaire focused on three issues: whether husbands and wives thought that unemployment had affected their health and, if so, whether treatment was being received, whether any impact on marital relationships was observed; and whether, using four indicators, unemployment was affecting the children in these families.

(a) *Health*

In both samples, the majority of couples (72% and 87%) reported that unemployment had had an adverse effect on the health of the husband and/or wife. The precise link between ill-health and unemployment is unclear, but, for many, unemployment is clearly stressful in itself, and to this must be added the physical and emotional strain of income deprivation.

Some indication of the cost of unemployment is given by the fact that significant numbers of male interviewees (16% in the 1st sample and 18% in the 2nd) were receiving treatment for mental and/or physical health problems which they attributed to worklessness. Moreover, as other studies have suggested, the strain on women appeared to be greater — 21% of wives in the 1st sample and 28% in the 2nd were, at the time of the interview, being treated for some illness which they related to their current circumstances. Once again, there is a difference between the 1st and 2nd samples.

The picture that emerged amongst this sub-group of households was one of depression, anxiety, ulcers and other stress-related disorders, alleviated by tablets and occasional admissions to psychiatric care. The following cases are fairly typical.

Mr and Mrs A: Mrs A suffers from agoraphobia and depression. She has been in the local psychiatric hospital recently. The husband also suffers from depression. Husband unemployed for more than 5 years.

Mr and Mrs B: Mr B, who is receiving treatment for depression and irregular sleeping habits, has been unemployed for more than 10 years.

Mr and Mrs C: Mr C is receiving treatment for neurosis and has been unemployed for more than 5 years.

Mr and Mrs D: Both are receiving treatment for stomach ulcers. Mr D has been unemployed for more than 5 years.

Mr and Mrs E: Mr E is receiving treatment for a nervous rash which emerged after redundancy. He has been unemployed for 5 years.

Mr and Mrs F: Mr F has been admitted to psychiatric care suffering from chronic depression and is still being treated. Mrs F is on valium for nervous anxiety.

Mr and Mrs G: Mrs G has received psychiatric treatment. She blames unemployment and increasing worries.

Mr and Mrs H: Mr H was in psychiatric care for six months with acute depression. According to his wife, 'he could not accept being out of work'. He had been unemployed for more than 2 years.

(b) *The perceived impact on marriage*

There was a close similarity between the two samples when interviewees were asked to assess the effect, if any, of unemployment on their marriages. In both samples, roughly three-quarters of couples reported a negative effect — only four couples felt that unemployment had brought them closer together. For the majority, unemployment and the consequent financial problems produced strain and tension.

Table 37: *Reported effect on marriage (%)*

	1st sample	2nd sample
Positive effect	1.2	1.4
Negative effect	75.2	79.2
No effect	22.8	18.0
Don't know	0.8	1.4

Once again, women appeared to be carrying the larger part of the strain, coping with both financial difficulties and damaged male egos — problems exacerbated in some cases by excessive drinking.

'He gets on my nerves sitting in the house. I can't wait to see him going out with the dog.'

'You fight and argue over stupid things that normally would not bother you.'

'It's constant arguments over financial matters. It irritates me to have him around the house all day. There's constant bickering over money.'

'It's emotional strain. Particularly at the beginning when my husband refused to register for unemployment for one year. Instead he worked as a part-time barman earning 30 quid a week.'

'At the beginning it caused a great strain, but we've grown accustomed to unemployment.'

'Presently he drinks heavily and this is putting a great strain on the fabric of the marriage.'

'He felt demoralised because I [wife] assumed the role of provider. It almost broke up the marriage — I was forced to give up my job.'

(c) Perceived effects on children

The effects parents thought unemployment was having on their children are indicated in Table 38. The majority of parents felt that their children were not suffering emotionally or making less progress at school than they might have done. However, cases of children not being able to attend school on occasion as a result of financial strain were not uncommon, and many children clearly could not fully participate in school life as a result of shortages of money in the family. It is noticeable that the 2nd sample appeared to be in more difficulty than the 1st.

Table 38: *Impact of unemployment on children (%)*

% reporting indicators I—IV	1st sample	2nd sample
I Progress at school affected	9.0	16.1
II Emotional distress	12.7	18.3
III Has missed school due to lack of shoes/uniform/bus fare	7.2	23.2
IV Unable to participate in school trips/outings	41.3	48.2

Receipt of free school meals was sometimes a focal point of stress and arguments at home. Whilst most were entitled to free school meals, in both samples 7% of families with children taking school meals were actually paying for them to avoid stigma.

The following are fairly typical of the comments made by parents where unemployment was thought to be having an effect.

'The boys lack incentive. They regard exams as a waste of time.'

51

'One of the girls dreads the coming of PE day — she has no gear as such and feels apart from the rest of the class.'

'The eldest girl is embarrassed when asked by teachers about her father's occupation.'

'Although the children are entitled to free school meals, they refused to take them. They felt degraded.'

'The children get upset when friends taunt them about their father being unemployed. They can't understand why their father is not working when the next-door neighbours are working.'

'The eldest girl is withdrawn and easily upset. Children taunt them when they are unable to go on holiday or participate in other activities.'

'The eldest boy got easily upset because he had to take free school meals. He was taunted by other children.'

'The eldest boy gets easily upset when he cannot participate in the activities of the other children.'

'The eldest boy is very conscious of father's unemployment. He feels isolated from the activities of other children, particularly during the summer.'

To sum up, the majority of marriages were reported to be under strain; significant minorities of both husbands and wives were receiving treatment for stress-related health problems; and significant numbers of children were feeling some effects of unemployment. The problem is clearly one of unemployment combined with poverty.

10 Perceptions, attitudes and life styles

It might be assumed that those out of work in an area of high unemployment would be more likely to have a positive view of themselves — to view their circumstances as arising out of a collective problem — and hence to sense a greater community understanding of their position. One might expect that unemployment in such a context would be less likely to be experienced as a matter for private shame, and that in areas where so many are on benefits the unemployed would be immune to 'scrounger-bashing'. It might also be expected that one would see at least the beginnings of a new life-style based on unemployment.

Comparison of our two samples suggests that to a degree, with regard to perception and attitudes, this may be the case. But even so, the large residue of feelings of stigma and failure that remains can hardly be considered healthy for either the individual or community. If this is the optimum level of adjustment, it can hardly be termed satisfactory. Moreover, there is little evidence of an alternative life-style being developed.

(a) *Perception of self*

Four indicators were used for assessment in this part of the interview: reported feelings of loss of self-confidence; feelings of being depressed most of the time; worry about being labelled a 'scrounger'; and feelings of loss of status in the community. Perhaps the most interesting aspect of the data collected is the differences between the 1st and 2nd samples.

Of those interviewed 45% reported feeling much less confident in themselves as a result of their experience of unemployment. This loss of self-esteem was much more pronounced among the 2nd sample; but even so, one-third of the 1st sample had the same response.

A similar, though narrower, gap appeared with regard to the proportion of each sample who felt that unemployment had deprived them of 'status or standing with other people'. On average, 60% thought that unemployment had reduced them in the eyes of others. Again, it did not appear that the length of unemployment was significant in accounting for the differences between the two samples.

Table 39: *Loss of self-confidence by duration of unemployment*

	1st sample	2nd sample
% of those unemployed under 2 years	30.4	76.9
% of those unemployed 2 years plus	31.2	80.7
Total as % of total sample	33.4	79.5

Table 40: *Reported loss of status by duration of unemployment*

	1st sample	2nd sample
% of total unemployed under 2 years	51.6	88.5
% of total unemployed 2-5 years	56.3	77.4
% of total unemployed 5 years plus	50.4	80.9
Total as % of total sample	52.8	79.4

Despite the high level of dependence on benefits generally in Northern Ireland, 57% of these unemployed men expressed anxiety that they might be labelled as 'scroungers' by the broader community. Once again, there was a clear difference between the attitudes of the two samples and, once again, it is perhaps surprising that so many still felt a risk of negative stereotyping.

Table 41: *Worry about being labelled a 'scrounger' by duration of unemployment*

	1st sample	2nd sample
% of total unemployed under 2 years	55.8	84.6
% of total unemployed 2-5 years	50.6	71.9
% of total unemployed 5 years plus	44.5	85.7
Total as % of total sample	49.2	79.7

In the light of this and other information, it is perhaps not surprising that the great majority of the men reported that they were depressed a lot or most of the time, and on this indicator there is little difference between the two samples (Table 42).

In all, only small minorities (6.8% 1st sample, 3.8% 2nd) did not score on at least one of these indicators; and in both samples, the majority scored on more than one of these. The 2nd sample was clearly more anxious — 83.5% felt that three or four of the indicators applied to them, compared with 40% of the 1st sample.

Table 42: *Depression by duration of unemployment*

	1st sample	2nd sample
% of total unemployed under 2 years	83.8	96.1
% of total unemployed 2-5 years	80.2	96.8
% of total unemployed 5 years plus	89.2	90.4
Total as % of total sample	84.8	94.9

(b) *Whose fault?*
It has been suggested in other surveys that unemployment is easier to cope with if the individual clearly perceives his/her worklessness as the result of external factors.[1] Our survey does not, however, give much support to this thesis.

Table 43 is of considerable interest for three reasons. First, when asked whom or what they felt to be responsible for their joblessness, those interviewed focused overwhelmingly on external factors. Second, there was no difference between the two samples. This is of interest as it might have been thought that those from the predominantly Catholic community would have referred to discrimination or past policies, and those from the predominantly Protestant community would have blamed the IRA or 'the troubles' generally. What is remarkable about this finding is that both sides appear to eschew local explanations and sectarianism, and instead attribute unemployment to the overall economic and social policies of the present government. This may represent a convergence of opinion worth examining more closely, for it is an unexpected result. Third, it is noticeable that blame is placed on government rather than the recession. Thus, there is a clear rejection, amongst these men at least, of government explanations for the present high unemployment. (It should be emphasised that this was a completely open-ended question.)

Table 43: *Perception of the causes of unemployment*

	1st sample	2nd sample
Mrs Thatcher/the government	57.6	72.2
Recession	15.2	—
Don't know	12.1	7.6
Own health/other problems	9.1	7.6
'The troubles'	1.9	5.1
Other	4.1	7.5

(c) *The worst aspects of being unemployed*

There was also a degree of agreement between the two samples on the worst aspects of being out of work. Our evidence supports other data from Northern Ireland and Britain, and indicates that any suggestion that the unemployed can 'settle down' to workless-ness and develop new life-styles — given time — bears little relation to reality. Despite the financial and other pressures on these men, boredom came top of the list of things disliked most about jobless-ness.

Table 44 indicates that boredom was mentioned by the majority of men in both samples. Once again, the duration of unemploy-ment does not seem relevant, but there is a difference between the two samples — men in the 1st sample were less likely than those in the 2nd to stress the problem of boredom. Nevertheless, those emphasising this problem constituted a majority in both groups.

Table 44: *Perception of worst aspects of being unemployed by duration of unemployment (%)*

Duration of unemployment	Boredom		Lack of money		Life finished		Other	
	1st	2nd	1st	2nd	1st	2nd	1st	2nd
— 2 years	50.7	76.9	43.4	38.4	5.8	—	8.6	3.8
2-5 years	59.2	65.6	37.1	56.2	12.4	—	3.4	3.1
5+ years	52.8	71.4	46.2	38.0	12.4	4.7	3.8	4.7
Total % of total sample	54.5	70.8	42.4	45.5	9.8	1.2	4.9	3.8

To supplement this data, a small group of men (10% of the total sample) were asked to complete time-sheets for a given day. The following are indicative of the picture of boredom and social isola-tion that emerged.

Mr A is a 26-year-old married man with two children. Prior to being made redundant, he was a plumber's mate, a job which he had held for three years.

AM

10.30   Get up.
11.00   Make breakfast for the wife and myself.
11.30   Go visit my mother.

PM

12.45   Return home to watch the one o'clock news.
 1.30   Play with the children.
 2.00   Listen to the radio or records.

4.30	Help the wife with the dinner.
5.15	Have dinner.
6.30	Go for a jog.
8.00	Watch television until bedtime.

Mr B is a 35-year-old married man with three children. He has been out of work for 16 months. Prior to unemployment, he worked in the construction industry for seven years.

AM

8.00	Get up.
8.15	Shave.
8.30	Help wife get the two youngest boys ready for school.
8.50	Take the boys to school.
9.15	Read the newspaper.
11.00	Do odds and ends about the house.

PM

1.00	Have a cup of tea and a sandwich.
2.30	Peel the potatoes for dinner.
3.15	Collect the children from school.
4.00	Watch television.
5.00	Prepare the dinner.
6.30	Potter about in the garden.
8.00	Watch television for the rest of the evening.
11.30	Bed.

Mr C is a 46-year-old married man with five children. He has been out of work for eight years. His previous employment was as a labourer.

AM

10.00	Rise.
11.00	Have breakfast.
11.30	Read the newspaper.

PM

1.00	Watch the news
1.30	Read newspaper.
2.00	Do the hoovering for the wife.
3.15	Prepare dinner.
5.00	Dinner.
6.00	Watch television until bed-time.

Thus, the main focal points of the day centred around taking the children to and from school and a limited range of activities around the house. The 'events' mentioned usually occupied a small portion of the day, stretched out to 'kill time'. The rest of the day was dominated by passive leisure pursuits, mainly watching television. The following are fairly typical comments:

'You are loafing about to try and find something to pass the time. You go out and dig the garden; but once that is finished, you have to try and find something else to do. Unless you dig the garden all over again!'

'All I do is sit here and stare out of the window, watching cars and people go by.'

'You lose contact with people — I seem to be more or less glued to the house.'

'It's not being able to have a decent life. It's like being in prison. Always locked up, no freedom.'

'It's always putting your hand in your pocket and finding nothing there.'

'There's nothing to look forward to. It's an inescapable situation.'

'I feel that I have failed as a human being.'

'You can't cater for the needs of your family, there's times you sit down and curse unemployment; it's hard on the heart and mind.'

The lack of involvement in local community projects or voluntary work may also be considered surprising, but perhaps the assumption that more people out of work means more people willing and able to undertake unpaid work is a crude one. Active participation in voluntary effort often costs money — there is the odd phone call to make and the socialising in the bar after meetings. Loss of self-confidence is less than conducive to taking on responsibility, and it is possible that the unemployed may resent and resist the assumption that they are available to work for nothing in a society that denies them paid employment.

(d) Perception of others unemployed

How did these men view others in the same position? Do they see others as at fault? To test this, the unemployed in both samples were asked if they agreed or disagreed with three statements.

Table 45 indicates that there was some, but not a great deal of, support for negative stereotypes of the unemployed amongst these unemployed men. What is of more interest here, perhaps, is the level of agreement between the two samples. Past research has suggested that in Northern Ireland 'scrounger bashing' is interlinked with sectarian prejudice.[2] A stronger reaction might, therefore, have been expected from the 2nd sample. The impact of the economic decline of the past seven years on both communities in Northern Ireland may account for this convergence of attitudes — if anything, the 2nd sample appears more liberal.

Table 45: *Perception of the unemployed (%)*

	Agree		Disagree		Don't know	
	1st	2nd	1st	2nd	1st	2nd
'A good lot of the unemployed wouldn't work anyway.'	23.7	15.6	67.7	77.9	8.6	6.5
'Most of the unemployed are doing the double (working on the side) anyway.'	20.2	17.3	48.3	53.3	31.5	29.3
'A lot of the unemployed are better off on the dole.'	35.2	22.1	54.8	74.0	10.0	3.9

(e) *The future*
To conclude this part of the questionnaire, interviewees were asked to assess their chances of obtaining employment. It is depressing to note that only small minorities in each sample (12% 1st sample, 10% 2nd sample) were very or quite optimistic that they would be back in work at any point in the future. The great majority (77% and 78%) thought that they had little or no chance of returning to work.

Summary

Four main conclusions can be drawn from this data. First, people with long experience of unemployment who live in communities with high unemployment rates do not seem to gain immunity from anxiety over the way others perceive their circumstances or from loss of self-esteem and feelings of demoralisation. Those for whom it is perhaps a newer experience culturally exhibit higher levels of concern; but, amongst those for whom it is not new, anxiety of one kind or another affects significant numbers. As a group they have not moulded new perceptions of their role and identity or acquired any certainty with regard to their right to support.

Second, these men generally blamed external factors for their unemployment, but this seems to have been cold comfort to them. Third, these men have not, in general, evolved a more collective, outgoing life-style. The picture that emerges is one of men isolated at home — the problem is a private one. Fourth, whilst there was some support for negative attitudes towards the rest of the unemployed, there was considerable disagreement with key statements.

References

1 R Marshall, 'The psychological effects of unemployment on men with dependent children', unpublished MSc thesis, Queen's University, Belfast.
2 E Evason, *Ends that won't meet*, CPAG 1980.

11 Aspects of the benefits system

In this section of the questionnaire it was decided to concentrate on a limited range of issues: claimants' knowledge and receipt of single payments, feelings about contacts with DHSS staff, attitudes towards the introduction of housing benefit (1st sample) and understanding of critical aspects of the scheme when it came into operation (2nd sample).

(a) *Single payments*
The data on single payments now, of course, have a special significance. In both samples, the majority of supplementary benefit claimants had heard of these (93% 1st sample, 94% 2nd sample). Moreover, the majority of claimants had received a single payment in the preceding year — 74% in the 1st sample and 63% in the 2nd. Table 46 demonstrates the range of needs being met.

Table 46: *Households assisted with single payments (%)*

	1st sample	2nd sample
Furniture	53.0	32.9
Bedding	46.0	15.1
Decorating materials	26.5	13.9
Floor covering	9.9	10.1
Maternity needs	9.9	6.3
Miscellaneous	18.7	3.7

In both samples, the main source of information on single payments was friends and relatives. In the 1st sample, 63% had heard of single payments in this way; the next most important source of information for this group was the resource centre in the area, accounting for 28% of those who knew of this benefit. Official sources of information appeared to have had very little impact. Only 6% of these claimants had heard of single payments directly from a DHSS officer and only 2% had learned of them from DHSS leaflets. The local resource centre had clearly had a fairly significant impact.

Without any equivalent service in their neighbourhood, 77% of claimants in the 2nd sample reported hearing of single payments through friends and relatives, whilst 13% had learnt of them from DHSS officers or leaflets.

Single payments were clearly an important addition to the resources of these claimants. It is difficult to envisage need on this scale being met largely through loans and counselling. Unless there is a significant increase in the scale rates, the proposals for a social fund can only mean a cut in the volume of support available.

(b) *DHSS staff*

At this stage of the questionnaire, claimants were asked how they felt about the DHSS staff they dealt with generally and those who had visited them. Taking both samples together, 17% found DHSS staff generally to be very or quite sympathetic. Less fulsomely, 43% of claimants thought they were 'all right', whilst 40% had found officers to be unsympathetic. With regard to visiting officers, however, the position was slightly better. More than a quarter of claimants (28%) had found officers to be very or quite helpful, and 45% thought they were 'all right' — 27%, however, had found officers to be unhelpful.

The majority of claimants in both samples, therefore, have a positive or neutral attitude towards the DHSS staff they have been in contact with. The dissatisfaction of claimants who had not found officers helpful was based on a small, recurrent number of themes.

'They don't help you. You have to fight for everything.'

'They treat you as a statistic, not a human being.'

'They degrade you, they behave like the police.'

'I would not apply for a single payment. They make you feel like a beggar. I would not go through the procedure.'

'They do not seem to understand. They think you are lying.'

'They humiliate you. They give you the impression that they are paying the money out of their own pockets.'

'They're uninformative. Keep you in the dark with regard to other benefits.'

'The attitude is terrible — they make you feel like a beggar.'

(c) *Housing benefit*

The 1st sample was interviewed in the months preceding the introduction of housing benefit. Accordingly, interviewees were asked how they felt about the move from payments to cover housing costs to rebates: 56% were strongly opposed to the idea; one-third were in favour of the change; whilst the remaining interviewees did not feel it would make any difference. So, the prospect of housing benefit had no particular support in the community.

Information on the actual operation of housing benefit was obtained for 77 households in the 2nd sample. Twelve of these were having their benefits reduced as a result of the presence of grown-up children; for four households, the result had been an 80% plus cut in benefit; and for the remaining households the cut averaged 28% of benefit.

The second aspect of the scheme to be examined was claimants' knowledge of their rights of appeal. Under the housing benefit scheme, there is a two-stage appeals procedure. Claimants have a right to make written representations for an internal review of the decision, and then, if they are still dissatisfied, to ask for a hearing by a review board. Of the 77 claimants questioned, 43 stated they were not aware of these procedures and rights. Basic information had clearly not got through to housing benefit claimants.

Finally, claimants in the 2nd sample were asked if they had experienced any difficulties in the transition to housing benefit. One-third (24) reported that the main difficulty they had had was in understanding the scheme — they did not know what was happening to their benefit and, as they were certificated cases, there was anxiety as to whether or not their rent was being paid for them and concern that arrears might be mounting up. In addition, five claimants had experienced other difficulties — one claimant, for example, had apparently been notified that he would have his rent and rates fully covered, and was then told he was in arrears. The matter was still being sorted out at the time of the interview.

Summary

This part of the interview indicated that single payments were a vital source of assistance — in both samples, the majority of claimants had obtained such payments in the recent past. With regard to contacts with local DHSS staff, the majority of claimants thought they were either sympathetic or, at least, 'all right'. Finally, the data with regard to housing benefit are a matter for concern. There is clear evidence of lack of awareness of important rights under the scheme.

12 Conclusion

This pamphlet represents part of the continuing effort by CPAG (NI) to highlight the severe and deepening problem of income deprivation in Northern Ireland. Its publication is timely, coinciding as it does with the fierce controversy which surrounds government proposals for fundamental changes in the social security system. For if any region constitutes a test case with regard to the adequacy of these proposals, it is Northern Ireland.

This fact has been grasped by the people of the province. Local politicians at opposite ends of the political spectrum have united against the Green Paper. The past four months have seen a vigorous campaign by trade unions, district councils, the women's movement and the voluntary sector against the Fowler review. The evidence presented in this pamphlet provides the key to understanding this rare display of unity. Handicapped for years by a unique combination of disadvantages — the lowest wages, the worst unemployment and the highest cost of living — the province will also suffer disproportionately from the cuts and revisions under discussion. The poorest region will be hit hardest by policies based on assumptions which are actually refuted by its people's experience.

The review of statistical and other data in the first part of this pamphlet draws attention to a number of issues. The fact that local government in any real sense of the word does not exist in Northern Ireland is significant in itself with regard to the administration of many benefits. More specifically, for example, it also renders the rationale in the Green Paper for limiting the rebate on rates to 80 per cent (to promote greater local accountability) simply irrelevant. That this should go unnoticed is remarkable — at least to the people who live in Northern Ireland.

The very heavy level of dependence on benefits in the region demonstrated in the first half of this pamphlet makes cuts in benefits a matter of concern not purely with regard to their impact on individual households. Thought must be and should have been given to the economic consequences in severely deprived regions of cuts in purchasing power. Northern Ireland certainly cannot afford the job losses that we fear will accompany computerisation of the benefits system, on top of the job losses that are likely to flow from the cuts in purchasing power in the local economy, which seem inevitable if all or part of the Fowler package is implemented.

It should also be apparent from the first half of this pamphlet that Northern Ireland's social security system has characteristics which may become universal should the social fund become a reality, with a system of loans replacing single payments under the SB scheme. As so many claimants are in receipt of very small weekly allowances, some provisions to recover such loans from other benefits will be needed. The Northern Ireland Payments of Debt Act is a model to hand. It demonstrates that social security systems can ensure that income deprivation results in private need — cutbacks in food and clothing — rather than public debt. Claimants and public employees can have their benefits and wages drastically reduced with no right of appeal to tribunals.

The circumstances of specific groups in Northern Ireland illustrate the inadequacy of, and superficial thinking behind, much of the Fowler review. Northern Ireland's pensioners are poorer and less likely to have occupational pensions than pensioners in Britain. Abolition or modification of SERPS will have particularly drastic consequences for the living standards of future pensioners in Northern Ireland. Only 46 per cent of the labour force is currently covered by occupational pension schemes. With more unemployment for so many decades the province has a higher proportion of people who will simply be left to the means test. The extent of low pay means that fewer of those in work will be able to make adequate provision for themselves. The greater degree of female dependence means that women in Northern Ireland have most to lose from the withdrawal of rights presently accorded under SERPS. On top of all this, again, there are broader economic considerations. As the Northern Ireland Committee of the Irish Congress of Trade Unions has stressed, greater reliance on the private sector will mean an outflow of capital from the province, as pensions companies do not have their headquarters in Northern Ireland. Northern Ireland has a greater proportion of small and medium-sized firms; the region will, therefore, have to bear disproportionately heavy administrative costs if a policy of semi-privatisation is pursued.

The problem is not, however, simply confined to any modification in pensions policy. The heart of the issue is that Northern Ireland will come off worst at so many points. The region with the densest concentration of low pay clearly has most to lose if cuts in standard housing benefit are made. Because families are, on average, larger in Northern Ireland, the cut in the real value of child benefit, and the loss of money paid directly to women for their children as a result of the transition to the family credit scheme, will have a particularly harsh impact. Furthermore,

65

families in Northern Ireland will lose disproportionately if the loss of entitlement to other benefits, notably free school meals, is either not compensated for or compensated for only on the basis of the average loss to households across the UK. The region with the highest unemployment and greatest percentage of young people in the population has most to lose from policies already enforced which cut housing benefit by assuming higher contributions from non-dependants and from proposals to cut back the housing benefit and supplementary benefit paid to the unemployed in the younger age groups. The region with the greatest dependence on single payments has most to lose from the introduction of the social fund.

The region that may be hit hardest is also the region which has the most cause to question much of present government thinking — specifically, the notion that jobs will materialise if benefits are cut and wages held down. In the latter part of the 1970s benefits in Northern Ireland were effectively cut by raising fuel prices. Wage levels have long been lower and still Northern Ireland has more unemployment than anywhere else in the UK.

The second part of the pamphlet focuses on the experience of unemployment in two areas of Derry. The first is a mainly Catholic community, whilst the area from which the second sample was drawn is predominantly Protestant. The evidence effectively challenges both the assumption that, in time, the unemployed can adjust to worklessness — especially if they live in areas of persistently high unemployment — and also some of the stereotyped views which the two communities in Northern Ireland hold of each other.

In both samples, the majority of the 343 men interviewed had been out of work for more than two years. From interviews conducted with these men, it is evident that those drawn from the predominantly Protestant area were coping less well than the Catholics. Why this is so is unclear — but perhaps because unemployment is a newer experience culturally, there is a poorer adjustment among this group. Nevertheless, the difficulties experienced by the Catholic families are so pronounced that if this represents the extent to which families can 'adjust', it cannot be seen as acceptable.

When looking at the extent of psychological adjustment to unemployment, feelings of loss of confidence, loss of status and depression were prevalent. There was also a high level of anxiety about being labelled a 'scrounger'. Despite the fact that these men generally blamed the government for their unemployment, being without work was still seen as a source of personal shame and failure. Boredom was considered the worst aspect of being unemployed, and the time-sheets completed by some of the men indicated a limited, passive life-style. In short, as a group, these men showed little sign of developing a positive attitude towards themselves or a new way of life to cope with unemployment.

The data on the impact of unemployment on health and the family suggested that wives were under more strain than husbands. They were more likely to report a deterioration in their health and more likely to be receiving treatment for stress-related health problems. Taken as a whole, in both samples, significant minorities of husbands and wives were being treated for such disorders. In both samples, the majority of couples reported that unemployment had resulted in increased marital strain. In addition, though considerable efforts were clearly being made by parents to protect their children from the effects of the father's unemployment, it was evident that these efforts were not wholly successful.

All these households were living on poverty line incomes and neither sample appeared to be 'managing' well. Thus, for example, the majority could not put money aside, borrowed regularly from friends and relations, and lacked essential items of clothing. The financial difficulties and shortages faced by these households are hardly surprising. The majority faced fuel costs accounting for more than 20% of their weekly incomes, while expenditure on food, fuel and housing costs accounted for more than 80% of the incomes of most households. In addition, the majority had debts of one kind or another.

Finally, the survey looked at some aspects of the benefits system, and some important points emerged from the data: notably, single payments were a vital source of assistance. It is difficult to imagine how these households will cope if these extra payments are abolished — what they will cut down on if a system of loans is introduced.

In conclusion, it has long been accepted that Northern Ireland is the poorest region in the UK. The purpose of this pamphlet has been to provide a more up-to-date summary of the position and also to argue that instead of being regarded as unique, Northern Ireland can, in many respects, be viewed as a region from which much can be learned.

The experience of the province provides an insight into the ways in which benefits systems can be distorted. Northern Ireland highlights the irrelevance of current proposals for change and the inadequacy of much of the thinking underlying them. Moreover, these proposals are, of course, based on an assumption that unemployment will not fall below 10% in the foreseeable future. If there is any region which demonstrates the costs of such an assumption to individuals, families and communities, it is Northern Ireland.